Technical Theatre

Technical Theatre

A PRACTICAL INTRODUCTION

Christine A. White

Lecturer in Drama, Loughborough University

A member of the Hodder Headline Group
LONDON
Co-published in the United States of America by
Oxford University Press Inc., New York

For my parents,
Margaret and Tony White

First published in Great Britain in 2001 by
Arnold, a member of the Hodder Headline Group,
338 Euston Road, London NW1 3BH

http://www.arnoldpublishers.com

Co-published in the United States of America by
Oxford University Press Inc.
198 Madison Avenue, New York, NY10016

The advice and information in this book are believed to be true and
accurate at the date of going to press, but neither the author nor the publisher
can accept any legal responsibility or liability for any errors or omissions.

British Library Cataloguing in Publication Data
A catalogue record for this book is available from the British Library

Library of Congress Cataloging-in-Publication Data
A catalog record for this book is available from the Library of Congress

ISBN 0 340 76211 X (hb)
ISBN 0 340 76212 8 (pb)

1 2 3 4 5 6 7 8 9 10

Production Editor: Jasmine Brown
Production Controller: Bryan Eccleshall
Cover Design: Terry Griffiths

Typeset in 9.25 on 13pt Lucida by Cambrian Typesetters, Frimley, Surrey
Printed and bound in Great Britain by MPG Books Ltd, Bodmin, Cornwall

What do you think about this book? Or any other Arnold title?
Please send your comments to feedback.arnold@hodder.co.uk

Contents

Preface

There is no one correct method of creating a theatre performance. There is a need, however, to recognise the technological revolution that has occurred in theatre production. The revolution in the use of new technologies and the application of theatre craft is the preserve of creative people. Theatre has always been interactive and technological innovations provide us with exciting possibilities for a wide variety of theatrical experiences. This book reviews a number of production stories, beginning with the creative process and viewing technical theatre as a creative art, in order to give the student an understanding of technical practice from both a historical and a contemporary perspective. As technology is continually evolving, my aim is to demonstrate the way in which a knowledge of the history of techniques can be usefully applied to theatre practice. Hence the thematic approach to this book.

During the twentieth century the importance of communication with an audience has become ever more important. It has been further complicated by the theory that an audience receives information in what might be described as 'texts' – other, that is, than the literary text of the playwright. This means that the lighting plot, the scenery, costumes and any other part of the complex delivery system of theatre can be viewed as a text which adds many layers to the depth of our understanding about the events unfolding before us. This has inevitably led to a questioning of what theatre is.

The drama of dynamic sequencing – the succession of moving images – has been realised in art, performance art, television, video and film. This dynamic sequencing is in fact a dominant form of theatre production and it is often the dynamic – the movement – which is efficacious, producing emotion and meaning. Innovation in theatre production comes from people whose training may be in seemingly diverse areas, such as electronics, engineering, art and design. The suggestions that theatre is an industrial process or that theatre has its own aesthetic which provokes pure feeling should not be seen as incongruous. The element of chance in the creation of any art form has been emphasised by performance practitioners such as the composer John Cage and the choreographer Merce Cunningham. These developments and attempts at understanding the creative process must be noted in the making of theatre. This idea was embodied in Fluxus, an international movement of artists, writers, film-makers and musicians, and is most pertinent to theatre, as the performance is live. The flux is caused by different people performing the same act again and again, repeating their work but without absolute precision. It is these deviations in performance that create a complex poetic, which we ignore at our peril.

The teaching of theatre studies has been damaged by an over-emphasis on theory, which has led to a prescriptive approach to theatre production. This, I believe, has led to atrophy, restricting our sense of play and resulting in productions playing to ever-decreasing audiences in theatres which have become more akin to museums than vibrant performance spaces. The difficulties in meeting funding criteria, further exacerbate the problems of those wishing to produce innovative theatre. In the United Kingdom funding applications have been dogged by the narrowness of Arts Council categories, making it impossible for artists to work broadly, using a number of techniques which fall into different categories – visual art, theatre, opera, musical theatre, performance art, combined arts. Such categories straitjacket a work before it has even begun.

Theatre performances still exist in a twenty-first-century world, because new types of theatre collaboration have been slow to attract the support they deserve. The acceptance of the need for traditional theatre spaces and auditoriums, as the place for new works to be played in, must be questioned. The fluid landscapes of multimedia, which combine, say, film and video with live performance, allow the artist to play with time. There is nothing new in experimentation with time, of course; it has occurred in different ways in previous periods of theatre production, but always with the use of theatre craft. Today there is no need to restrict ourselves to purely traditional methods: as Robert Lepage suggests, 'The theatre is implicitly linked to technology. There is a poetry in technology, but we try to use it in a way that does not eclipse the action on stage.' (Rush, 1999, p. 70) The work of Lepage's company Ex Machina encompasses large-scale theatre and the use of multimedia formats. Primarily, then, the use of technology must enhance the communication of the story to the audience. A successful marriage between traditional stagecraft and new technologies promises vivid and exciting performances for theatre-makers and theatre-goers alike.

How to use this book

Throughout the text technical words have been set in bold type; these are defined in the text or in special boxed inserts. Some exercises are provided to enable the student to create his or her own response to the context, aesthetic and technology that has been discussed, and a Bibliography and Further Reading list is given at the end of the book. The book contains both Metric and Imperial measures: there are areas of technical theatre where Imperial measures are still used, for example when ordering sheets of plywood. Here is a basic conversion chart to help you with your work. Any errors with reference to definitions pertaining to theatre remain the author's sole responsibility.

1 cm = 10 mm = 0.394 in	1 g = 1000 mg = 0.035 oz
1 m = 100 cm = 1.034 yd	1 kg = 1000 g = 2.205 lb
1 in = 2.54 cm	1 oz = 28.35 g
1 foot = 12 in = 30.48 cm	1 lb = 16 oz = 0. 454 kg
1 yd = 36 in = 91.44 cm	

Acknowledgments

Great thanks are due to all those technically creative people with whom I have been lucky enough to work and who continue to be a source of inspiration and excitement. In particular, I would like to thank Marsha Roddy, Bettina Reeves, Phil Engleheart, Adrian Rees and Jenny Carey. It will also be apparent on reading this book that the writer and director Nona Shepphard has been integral to the artistic experiences which we have all been encouraged by her to share: I would like to take this opportunity on behalf of myself and my colleagues to thank her for her openness and her inspiring working relationship.

Introduction to the context of theatre-making

There are many ways of making theatre and this is a fact to be celebrated, yet it can cause a great amount of confusion and irritation amongst students, as they try to create their own pieces of work. One reason for this frustration is the need to pinpoint particular solutions to particular problems which inevitably arise during the planning of any production. Creative solutions and theatrical techniques are often sought not only to solve practical problems but to create moments of theatricality – the transformations and imaginative leaps we wish our audience to embark upon and enjoy. So it is with some consternation that we may seek a solution to a particular staging problem, as there are so many options for the resolution of such problems and they are dependent on aesthetic choices – considerations of style, context and meaning. This is where the technology of theatre and technical knowledge collide with artistic and aesthetic vision. Very often this collision has to take place in the minds of the technicians, for it is they who offer up ideas for solutions, very often attempting new techniques based on sound theatrical practice, but taking into account current **Health & Safety** requirements, combined with the ultimate aim of the moment, the performance and the desired audience response. This vast array of skills means that technical theatre requires an understanding of what is meant by theatricality, spectacle, effects, conceits, transformations, and so on. It also requires an understanding of solutions which may fall into different theoretical practices. For example, the German poet and dramatist Bertolt Brecht (1898–1956) developed a new style of 'epic' theatre and a new theory of theatrical alienation, which relies on the audience's reflective detachment rather than the production's atmosphere and action. (His works include *The Threepenny Opera* [1928] and *The Caucasian Chalk Circle* [1948].) Other theoretical influences include modernism, naturalism, and heightened realism.

In addition, we must understand the varied contexts of theatre-making; whether the performance takes place in a theatre building,

Health & Safety (Health Service Executive)

In all areas of theatre there are particular practices which can be dangerous. The theatre is an industrial workplace and you will be working with public access and electrical equipment. The HSE is recognised in the UK as the rules which protect workers in the workplace. Each theatre building will usually have a copy displayed in a prominent place. You must abide by the rules and, above all, follow safe working practices. **Health & Safety** considerations are covered in each chapter, as we discuss the use of space and equipment.

specifically constructed for theatre performances, or, for example, in a castle or an office. The techniques and practices of technical theatre allow for the creation of a special place for performance, which can be controlled and manipulated to encourage an audience response.

A brief history of technical theatre

The systems of communication and methods used in technical theatre have, like so many industrial practices, grown out of many years of development and transformation. The aesthetic choices made for medieval theatre and for Elizabethan theatre reflect the stage-craft of the day and the technical solutions then available. During the period covered by medieval drama, some six hundred years ago, a number of staging devices were used. For example, **pageant wagons** gave height, which enabled a large crowd to see the performance, and could travel from town to town, and move to different locations within a town. **Mansion Houses** or **Booths**, originally static locations usually in a line which had scenic elements for the performance of the Christian scriptures and an **in the round** formation, which had the audience surrounding the action of the performance.

The purpose-built open-air theatres of the Elizabethan period developed from other outside entertainments which managed a large audience in a relatively small space. These theatres provided non-specific locations but in their architectural arrangement they offered levels and domestic locations such as balconies and inner rooms. In both medieval drama and the drama played on the Elizabethan stage, startling effects were achieved, such as **Hell Mouth**, which blew fire and smoke, **cranes** which enabled actors and objects to fly, and **trap doors** for sudden appearances and disappearances. Stages were places which had the possibility of producing illusions and they developed out of the aesthetic of the time. Some methods and technologies may have changed but often the systems that have a proven record remain as 'best practice' even though their heritage may belong to the nineteenth century or even long before. It is this area, in particular, which can be confusing. However, at each stage of this book you will find notes explaining the heritage of particular practices and how developments have changed that practice. In addition, there are highlighted areas which offer solutions to common problems. Naturally, this book cannot cover all eventualities but with

Theatre in the round

The first records we have of theatre in the round are from the medieval period. We should also remember, however, that public entertainment at the **Colosseum** in Rome was in the round. The audience, surrounding the action, did not have a unified line of vision. In contemporary staging the settings tend to be restricted to small units, for example furniture and props, or symbolic features, which do not impede the view of one section of the audience over another. It is commonly thought that theatre in the round has a greater sense of ritual and ceremony. Some theatre theorists believe this form includes a greater active participation of members of the audience because they are continually reminded of the presence of one another.

Stephen Joseph (1927–67) was a pioneer of theatre in the round in Britain. He toured towns which had no theatre building, setting up his shows in the round. In 1962 he set up the first theatre in the round in Stoke-on-Trent.

some lateral thinking you should be able to apply your knowledge. The practice of lateral thinking is the key to the use of technologies in any age of the theatre. It is the effective application of techniques which produces desired effects. Very often you will need to research and practise solutions to staging problems. Even new productions of a text from an earlier period will involve you in a certain amount of research and development, which, in turn, will inevitably inform your practice.

Theories about sound production and ideas about the best way to reproduce vocal and other sound effects have resulted in the development of specific styles of theatre building. The arrangement of the auditorium not only affects the audibility of the performers but theatre architecture can also affect the nature of the relationship between performer and audience. Often actors, certainly contemporary actors, have clear views as to the best 'feel' of a performance space, regardless of the age the theatre building or style of the space. The performance space will always have a direct bearing on what is performed in it. Most important is the arrangement of an audience in relation to the performance. The reception of the product depends on the nature of the audience's position and the ways of staging should be considered in direct relation to how the audience is seated. The choices are endless, but some popular relationships of audience to performance are: **end on**, where the audience directly faces the performance; **in the round**, where members of the audience surround the performance, viewing it from all sides, and are simultaneously aware of their own presence; **amphitheatrical**, a semicircular arrangement, which if squared off becomes a three-sided theatre environment or **thrust stage**. It is also possible to create such arrangements within any open-air space or in a hall. In fact, Italian architect Sebastiano Serlio (1475–1554) suggested ways in which one might do this in his book *L'Architettura* published in 1551. Here Serlio set out how an open space could be converted into a successful auditorium.

Most of our modern scenic practices stem from this period, but also from the references to stage scenery made by the Roman architect Vitruvius (first-century BC), whose ten volume work *De architectura* had a major influence on Renaissance architects. Here we learn of the types of scenic units which were used during the reign of Augustus (27 BC – AD 14), one of the most useful being the **periaktoi**, a triangular unit which could revolve to show three different scenes. We do not know how this unit was constructed but it is likely that it was made of wood and then painted. The scene change would have occurred simply by lifting the periaktoi and turning it, or by turning it on a cylinder.

Serlio used cloth-covered frames for scenery very similar in construction to the

Thrust Stage

The **thrust stage**, as its name implies, 'thrusts' the stage into the auditorium and places the performance amongst the audience, and allows a much larger audience to be seated closer to the stage than other seating arrangements. Usually the front rows follow the lines of the stage; the less sharp the lines of the stage, the more this arrangement becomes like an amphitheatre. One drawback for productions requiring large scenic units, such as flying pieces, lies in the problem of blocked sightlines for individual members of the audience. The heritage of this stage form dates from the Elizabethan playhouse, but is evident also in the use of wagons, and even planks and barrels, to make a raised platform which an audience surrounds.

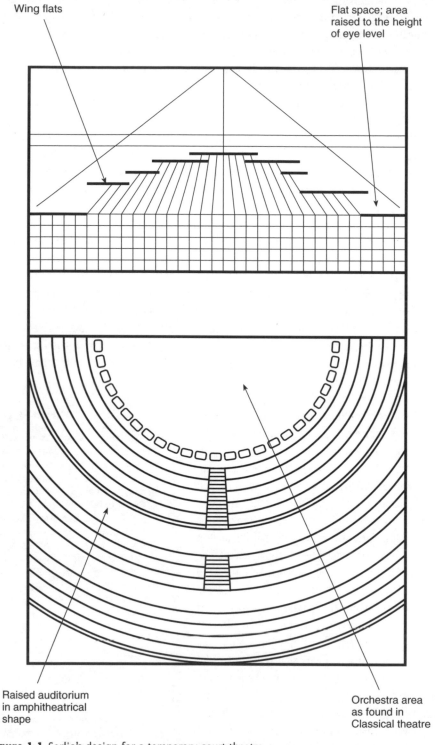

Wing flats

Flat space; area
raised to the height
of eye level

Raised auditorium
in amphitheatrical
shape

Orchestra area
as found in
Classical theatre

Figure 1.1 Serlio's design for a temporary court theatre

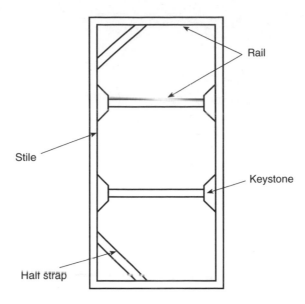

Figure 1.2 The flat frame is usually supported by a brace, a hooked pole held in place by a weight.

method by which canvas was stretched on wooden frames for oil paintings. In 1551 the Italian painter and art historian Giorgio Vasari (1511–74) commented on the benefits of this innovation: 'In order to carry pictures from one place to another, men have invented the convenient idea of painting on canvas, which, weighing very little, can be rolled up, and easily transported from place to place.' It is not known when these frames were first used, but by 1630 the English architect and theatrical designer Inigo Jones (1573–1652) had developed the cloth-covered frame or **flat**.

This form of scenic unit dominated the English stage for nearly three hundred years. Modern staging employs many different kinds of scenic device and mostly painted canvas flats are no longer in use, at least in the way described by Vasari. However, set construction does owe a great deal to the application of techniques which are used to create flats.

Another feature which has revolutionised theatre production is the way in which objects, scenes and people began to be suspended from above the stage. This too was developed in classical times, most notably for the arrival of the gods who were lowered by Crane from the **scene house**, at the back of the orchestra, the main performance area. The scene house stood behind the performance area and formed a backing to the events played out in front. The 'orchestra' literally meant the large area in front of the scene house which was used predominantly for dance by the chorus in Greek drama. The crane mechanism gave rise to the term **deus ex machina**, literally, 'god out of a machine', and refers to that point in a play when a god is introduced to resolve the plot. The notion of flying was also apparent in medieval theatre practice in Britain and in Europe. It is believed that the flying of people and objects took place in Renaissance playhouses, such as the Globe on the south bank of the Thames in London. The successful operation of these devices depended on available technology to provide practical solutions to theatrical problems.

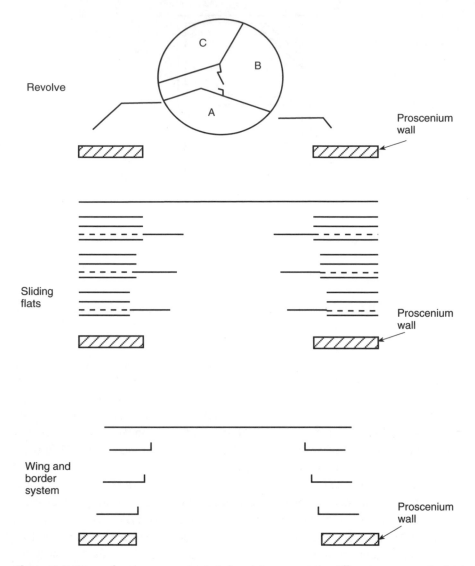

Figure 1.3 Types of scenery movement: A, B and C represent the different scenes on the 'pie' of the revolve.

The nature of these mechanisms and their complexity changed in the seventeenth century with the advent of the court masques, designed by Inigo Jones. The techniques developed for the masques were to dominate the construction, rigging and handling of scenic elements for the next two hundred years. The seventeenth-century stage comprised a series of **wings**, which were created by flats on either side of the stage. The change of scene was possible by sliding back each wing towards offstage to reveal new wings behind. At the same time the **backcloth** was raised to the ceiling, also known as **the flys**, to reveal another cloth with a new scene painted on it. The side flats were pulled along grooves in the stage floor, and as many as six different scenes could be revealed in succession.

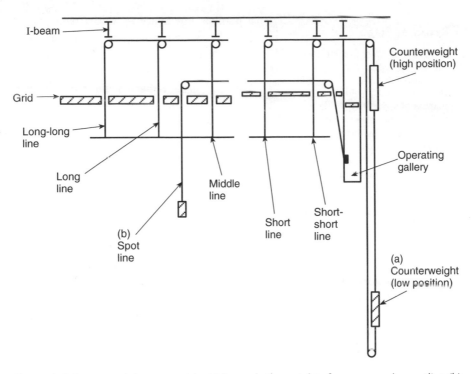

Figure 1.4 Counterweight system (a) which equals the weight of scenery, and a spotline (b) with no counterweight.

By the nineteenth century the larger theatres had replaced the grooves with slots. Manipulated beneath the stage floor, the flats fitted into the slots and moved on wheels (**chariots**) to facilitate an indefinite number of scene shifts. In order to make the chariots move more smoothly and with less effort, and therefore less manpower, **winches** were added to the system. A combination of winches and **counterweights** were devised to lift the framed backcloth into the flys, and relied on the use of **hemp** rope to lift and move the heavy scenic pieces.

This type of scenery had many benefits, allowing as it did for rapid scene shifts. However, it limited the stage arrangement and therefore the design of scenery, to one basic type of setting – end-on flat-scene staging.

In the late eighteenth century, as this machinery was developing, steamships had begun to replace sailing ships for the transportation of goods. The changes in technology in seafaring meant that many seamen and riggers for the sailing ships were out of work. This was the theatre's good fortune, as it was becoming more labour intensive with the use of large set pieces. Unemployed seamen found work as casual labourers in the theatres, usually shifting scenery, and they set about solving theatrical problems by using their sailing knowledge. Their skills in the use of ropes to lift and manoeuvre cargo, together with their head for heights, explains why ropes and knots are so important to the development of the theatre and to theatre practice today. This is why hemp sets became so common, using counterweights and cleats to tie off ropes, as well as pulleys

---

Revolving Stage

Karl Lautenschläger first introduced a revolving stage at the Residenztheater in Munich in 1896. This mechanism provided rapid changes of scene by splitting the circle of the **revolve** into 'pie' sections which fitted the proscenium opening. The Olivier stage at the Royal National Theatre, London, has a **drum revolve**, which not only revolves on a horizontal plane but can rise up from the stage floor or drop down below the stage level.

---

and other ironmongery, which could just as easily be found in a ship's chandlery as a theatre (flying is discussed in Chapter 9).

History, however is not a linear progression of ideas but rather a mixing of old and new ideas at a certain time, and during the late nineteenth and early twentieth centuries the German theatre pioneered new developments in stage machinery. The style of theatre was influenced by the way in which people were developing ideas current in philosophy and also in art. This particularly related to ideas of perception and therefore philosophies of realism. Theatre practitioners wished to use three dimensional objects as more realistic presentations rather than painted representations and these structures were very heavy. **Stage lifts** were designed to enable changes of scene and creating some surprising moments; in particular, the arrival or disappearance of ghosts. The advancing technologies of steam and hydraulics enabled the same effects to be created by using differently powered systems. The theatre adapted the new technology, using the new mechanisms which had been introduced to domestic and industrial areas. As a result, the mechanisms of the theatre space and specific theatre buildings at the beginning of the twentieth century reflected the industrial processes in production and manufacturing. The stage was a mass of levers, elevators, **turntable revolves** and **moving platforms**. However, few theatre buildings could house all these devices and few theatre companies could afford to support a staff to maintain and operate them. Furthermore, the idea that theatre required all these innovations was far from being proved. The use of technologies, rigidly set down as general practice, can be just as limiting to the imagination of the designer and the audience as the wing and groove system had become during the theatre's earlier technical history. Nevertheless, there are some areas of theatre production where the debt to technology should not be underestimated. For example, the developments in lighting technology have been of major importance.

The earliest lighting operator was the candle-snuffer, who trimmed the candles in the early indoor theatres to stop them guttering and going out. At the end of the performance they were allowed to keep the remains of any candles as a perk of the job. In the sixteenth century Serlio was innovative in the use of lighting effects, which were later refined by Inigo Jones. Serlio wrote:

> . . . if you need a great light to shew more than the rest, then set a torch behind, and behind the torch a bright basin, the brightness whereof will shew like the beams of the sun . . . You may also place certain candlesticks above the scene, with great candles burning therein, and above the candlesticks you may place some vessels with water, wherein you may put a piece of camphor, which burning, will throw a very good light, and smell well.
>
> (Nagler, 1952: 79)

Flaming torches, candles and burning oil were all used to great theatrical effect. Jones used candles and reflectors to enhance the splendour of his scenic arrangements and in the court masques he experimented with the use of candles flown in and out to suggest the quality of dimming and illumination. It was not until the nineteenth century and the advent of the gaslight, however, that dimming in theatres could be achieved with relative ease. At that time the gas table (the main intake for the gas to the backstage area) was controlled by a series of taps. The job of illumination was undertaken by the head gas man, who had a team of gas men scurrying about the backstage areas, adjusting the taps to raise and lower the flames, thus adjusting the flames' colour and brightness. The most notable director who used gaslight to great effect was the English actor Henry Irving (1838–1905). As manager of London's Lyceum Theatre, he would plot through his productions, requiring lighting changes at certain points in the performance, using the light to heighten the dramatic effect. Armed with these directions, the head gas man would cue his workers. The potential danger of gas escaping or remaining unlit from an outlet is obvious. In fact, accidents did happen and many theatres burned down. **Limelights**, which also had the potential to burn down a theatre, enabled actors to be individually lit on stage, and were used for special effects. The operation of the limelight was a skilled job.

Over a long period the positioning of lighting units followed the same pattern. As the technology changed from oil to gas to electricity the unit positions remained unchanged as they were the most suitable for the lighting of scenery from the wings and from above. They can therefore still be referred to as **wing lights**, which are situated at the sides of the stage, lighting the scenery; **footlights**, lighting from the front of the stage and at stage floor level, and **floodlights** overhead on bars and what was described as a **follow spot**, a lantern which could be moved while lit to follow the performer. This light was the direct descendant of the limelight which burned lime to produce the light. It was not until the latter part of the twentieth century that it was possible to place lighting units in more or less any position in relation to the performer and the audience.

The first theatre to use electricity was the Savoy in London and the positive or negative effects of this technology on the nature of the theatricality that was created were much discussed at the end of the nineteenth century. As the technology developed, so the means of operation changed. In early theatre candle snuffers were seen on stage – in court masques they were choreographed and costumed into the performance. As the technology developed so did the ways in which the units for lighting were placed around the performance area. Initially, the people who raised or lowered the flames of the lights needed to be near to those units. However, as large electrical dimmers were developed, the units were placed backstage. Often operated from under the stage, the need for operators to be cued to make a lighting change was ever greater if the effects were to be synchronised with the drama on the stage. Similarly, the scenic changes created with flats and flying systems were now also carried out by operatives who could no longer see the whole effect of their operation. The need for someone to manage these changes and co-ordinate the sequences of change became paramount, and resulted in the development of the role of stage manager.

Theatre sectors, their constitution and theatre-making

There are of course very different types of theatre company: a building with technicians and administrative staff but no actors; an office with an administrator and an artistic director; an artist or actor who works alone and sells productions to other companies. The word 'company' can also refer simply to a group of actors. What constitutes a theatre company is dependent on the way in which that company is funded. Theatre is a commercial venture, requiring payment for the entertainment it provides. However, unlike most commercial enterprises, many theatres today are funded by the Arts Council. This programme of state subsidy began after the Second World War and was instituted by the English economist John Maynard Keynes (1883–1946), who was responsible for the first Arts Council of Great Britain (ACGB) and its initial charter, 1945–50. He set up the means by which the government would pay for some of the arts activity in the country, which had been so important for morale during the war. The civilian arts unit, the Committee for the Encouragement of Music and the Arts (CEMA), and the armed forces entertainment corps, the Entertainments National Service Association (ENSA), were amalgamated in order to bring under one organisation a provision for the arts which was centrally funded. Before the war privately run theatre companies toured the country, and played in London and the larger cities. However, when the war was over much of the commercial circuit had closed due to financial pressures. The inauguration of the ACGB was able to provide for a circuit of venues, and as a result, a theatre was built in most cities in Britain as part of the post-war rebuilding and civic pride programme. This led to a system of organisation which grew into an established series of **repertory houses** – building-based companies which produced their own work – and **receiving houses**, which accepted work from a growing number of itinerant theatre companies. In return for public funding both types of theatre strove to be as commercial as possible, while the subsidies offset part of the production costs, thus keeping ticket prices low. This principle was thought to benefit the whole community by providing theatre which would both stimulate and entertain the general public.

Within these arrangements it is clear that the venues for performance and the itinerant companies producing work for these venues would have different structures and different technical needs. The architecture of theatre buildings directly affected the products that were created, and to a certain extent the expectations of what was to be presented in each type of venue resulted from the style and layout of the auditorium. The size of theatre auditoriums and the size of the stage has changed dramatically over the centuries and there are many theories as to the best dimensions and relationships of performer to audience. Lee Simonson (1950) suggests that the total width of the stage floor should be at least twice, preferably three times, that of the **proscenium** opening, in order that an actor who leaves to the right of the stage and has to appear a minute later at the left should not be impeded in his movements. In *Why Not Theaters Made for People* Per Edstrom discusses a more spiritual approach to the correct proportions of performance spaces. He relies on the translation of Vedic scripts which, within the precepts of ancient Indian philosophy, describe the performance space in relation to the size and shape of human beings. (In this theory all measurements are calculated from the length of a person's forearm.) A sacred geometry is thus formed, a geometry which one can find in a number of ancient religions and philosophies. Conversely, in *Architecture, Actor and Audience* Iain Mackintosh discusses the theory of theatre space in relation to proportions which support the performer, and remarks on the surprising nature of older playhouses which achieve this by surrounding the performer with audience.

That there are so many thoughts on the nature of the relationship between audience and performer is proof of the need to consider what is most appropriate for your theatre work and how the images and settings you present change the context of that performance. There is strong evidence to suppose that the different performance reactions are actually created in the viewing undertaken by the audience. Indeed, Eric Bentley in the *Theory of the Modern Stage* highlights ideas of modern makers of theatre, whilst Martin Esslin in *The Field of Drama* discusses the processing of information by a more scientific means, in order to understand the audience and the process of the creation of theatre. Both writers endeavour to look at the general principles that may go towards an understanding of theatre and an understanding of the making of theatre.

Proscenium Arch

The word 'proscenium' derives from the Greek *proskenion*, from *pro-* (before) and *skene* (scene), and refers to the arch or opening which separates the stage from the auditorium. In his court masques, Inigo Jones was the first to use the **proscenium arch** in England. This architectural feature has developed over the last two centuries as a picture frame through which the audience views the performance, and was particularly popular in the nineteenth century. This form of staging allows the audience to see many scene changes and spectacular transformations because the mechanisms by which the changes occur are hidden behind the proscenium wall and the wing space at the sides. Such theatres usually have a **fly tower**, which houses the **flying bars**, **winches** and **motors** to facilitate scenic changes. Generally in these auditoriums it is desirable to further conceal the mechanisms by flying **masking**, which blocks the angle of vision, or **sightlines**, from the auditorium into the wings and up into the flys.

The status and contribution of technicians

The status and role of theatre technicians are often dependent on the type of theatre being created. One can, of course, create theatre in any number of spaces – for example, in a street or town square, where technology may or may not be needed. For example, the busker playing acoustic guitar has different needs from the street violinist who uses a microphone, drum machine and tape deck with an amplifier to produce a backing track to his or her solo performance. The use of technology can create a very different effect and thus a different kind of performance. The choice is based on the performance requirements and aesthetic preferences, in this case made by the performer. As soon as a number of performers have gathered there is often a need for co-ordination, so technical theatre is not just about technology but is also about stage management. A successful co-ordination will lead to the vivid creation of an illusion. Going back to our violinist, the technical knowledge to create a well-balanced piece of amplified music does take some time to learn and practise, if in playback good quality is to be achieved. The knowledge required to make certain theatrical choices increases in direct relation to the complexity of the job in hand. Most of us are continually learning new approaches, and new ideas combine the application of old and new techniques. It is our receptiveness to learning which is most important. It is worth considering how you might improve on what you have achieved at each stage of the technical process. If your work is created to tour, then these improvements are vital. It is important to try to perfect your show: the ease with which it can be set up and taken down will impact dramatically on the access to different venues and performance spaces. In this process it is vital to maintain a sense of what is the best aesthetic and to avoid cutting or dispensing with those features that make your theatrical presentation distinctive.

CHAPTER 2

The Repertory System

Case Study

A Passionate Woman by Kay Mellor
- Leicester Haymarket Theatre (1999)
- Director: Nona Shepphard
- Designer: Adrian Rees
- Lighting: Christine White

The Text

A Passionate Woman tells the story of Betty, a woman in her fifties, on the day of her son Mark's wedding. During the course of the play she reflects on her life and past loves, and conjures up the ghost of her lover Craze, Mark delays his wedding, and she decides that her life needs to change. The play ends with Betty flying off in a hot air balloon, waving to Mark, Craze, and her husband Donald.

Technical Challenges

The action takes place in the attic and on the roof of a semi-detached house somewhere in England. When Betty is on the roof the fire brigade is called and Mark steers an electric extendable ladder up to the roof to rescue his mother; he falls and clings to some broken guttering. He is rescued by the ghost of Craze, by appearing to slide on his back from the bottom of the roof to the top. Donald buys Betty a surprise balloon ride and flies in with the balloon to collect her from the roof. When Betty flies off in the balloon on her own, father and son descend on the electric extendable ladder.

Prior to meeting the Haymarket Theatre staff, Nona Shepphard, Adrian Rees and I met to discuss the play. Adrian Rees had designed a white card model of the set and the team talked through the plot in relation to the set and how it needed to work for the story to be told. In the play text we see the attic and, through the skylight, the exterior of the roof, and finally the action moves outside to the roof with chimney. It was agreed that all these places should be in view, as well as the entrance to the attic, as there had to be a sense of tension developing from the characters' fear of climbing onto the roof, clinging to it for some time, almost falling from it, and then being rescued either by ordinary or supernatural means. The angle of the roof became crucial – too flat and it would not look real or dangerous, too steep and it could really cause an accident. At the same time,

Figure 2.1 Scene from *A Passionate Woman*; note the curved cyclorama.

it was essential to create a credible illusion of Craze's ghost, which could walk with ease on the roof and even do a dance routine on it.

The design solution to these activities was to use a turntable stage, or revolve. This meant that the different locations of attic, attic and roof, and whole roof could be shown relatively easily. It also meant that the revelation of each location was a dramatic surprise to the audience. The scale of the house roof filled the stage's proscenium opening. Behind it, to maintain the illusion, were chimney stacks with television aerials and tree tops. Since the entrance for the actors was through the attic hatchway, they accessed the sets from the **substage**, beneath the stage floor, and because the revolve would be in use there had to be three floor traps in the stage to provide access to the three stops of the revolve, the attic, attic and roof, and roof.

The house was cut away and the attic was strewn with **found properties** (props from theatre stock), which were appropriate to the period and the age of the people who lived in the house. For example, we see Mark's much-loved, now discarded, cuddly rabbit. This prop was not written into the text of the play but became significant for Betty, who holds the toy as she talks of her youth. A 1950s record player was used as a **practical prop** because it was necessary that the turntable was seen to go round. The music, in fact, was pre-recorded and was played through a small speaker located within the record player, the sound to be gradually faded into other speakers on stage and in the auditorium.

Properties

A **property (prop)** is defined as any item which is not built into the set. Props can be made, bought, borrowed or hired. **Rehearsal props** are temporarily used in rehearsal as substitutes for the items which will be used in performance. **Personal props** are those items for which an actor takes full responsibility – like a pen or handkerchief, watch or ring, which may be worn or used during the production. **Practical props** are those which are 'real', in that they do the job for which they were designed, for example a table lamp that illuminates when switched on, or a gun that fires when the trigger is pulled.

The revolve was not part of the stage architecture in the Haymarket, and in this production the attic space was built to revolve rather than the stage floor. The movement was powered by an electric motor. In order for the drive unit to work, the scenic piece has to have enough pressure on the stage floor for the wheels under it to grip. This is called a friction drive. It is the contact of the two surfaces which drives the wheels forward.

The hot air balloon had to appear on stage and land on the roof for Donald to disembark and Betty to climb into it and fly out. The balloon's basket and the material of the bottom half of the balloon itself was cheated, that is, we did not make the full balloon above the basket but merely used enough material to suggest that the balloon itself went up beyond the proscenium opening and out of view. However, those people sitting in the auditorium with the worst sightlines, that is, the first few rows, who could see up into the flys to the mechanisms of the theatre and offstage theatre spaces, would not have had the same sense of the reality of the balloon. This is a prime example where masking was important, not just for the look of the stage but for the concealment of a scenic piece which in the course of the play should not be seen until its moment of entry.

A smoke machine was sited in the basket and the actor pressed the trigger to release smoke as the balloon descended; the sound of the smoke machine reinforced the effect. The movement of the balloon had to be carefully controlled – it had to track on stage from stage right to centre stage and also drop in at an angle. This involved running two tracks and motors, one which could manage the horizontal movement and the other to deal with the vertical movement. Both motors had variable speed, so the horizontal movement could occur more quickly than the vertical movement or vice versa, which helped to give the impression that the balloon was flying. There was one operator and this manoeuvre took a great deal of skill, as there was no way of marking the correct speed for either motor except by eye. The skills required were similar to that of clutch control on a car, remembering that the operator had to land the balloon on the roof in order that an actor could safely leave the basket and another actor get in. The motors used were called turfers. The technical specifications on these motors show the optimum weight that the tracks and motors can be loaded with.

Another unusual scenic feature was the extendable ladder from the fire engine. For the spectacle of the show, and the style of the production which was realistic, the ladder needed to be a motorised unit with a cage which could take two people. The cost to buy or hire such a unit for the duration of the run was prohibitive, so this production negotiated a sponsorship deal from a company which hired motorised ladder units. Commonly known as cherry-pickers, these units have a wheel base which can be driven to any location, then by adjusting the controls the ladder extension can be raised and turned. For insurance purposes, the actor who was to drive the ladders in the show had to receive the same training as the technicians. Again, without being able to see the movement, the actor had to learn how to drive the ladders to the correct position in the orchestra pit and back round again to exit the stage.

The last challenging scenic device was the means by which Mark could fall from the apex of the roof to the gutter and seem to hang there until he is rescued by Craze, who, without touching Mark, gets him back up to the apex of the roof. The magical movement of Mark's sliding upwards to the top of the roof was technically spectacular. The sense of danger was very present in the precarious angle of the roof and the 2-metre drop to the orchestra pit. Furthermore, the actor was already on an incline, the beginning of which was 50 cm above the stage floor, while the apex of the roof was 3 metres from the stage floor. The mechanism devised to pull the actor back up the roof was a harness and steel-wire line. The line dropped through the roof and over a pulley to a hand winch. With the attic in view, the winch was hidden in the chimney breast. The actor put the harness under his wedding suit in the interval, as the fall and rescue occurs in Act 2. The actor hooked a small ring from the harness onto a line which was located on the roof. The director and actors worked together to disguise the moment he clips himself on and this was achieved by distracting the attention of the audience to his mother. When asked, many in the audience were unaware that the actor was wearing a safety harness when he tumbled down the roof, coming to a stop at the guttering. A few moments later the guttering gives way under his weight, or at least that was the illusion. This piece of guttering was on a hinge and each night was re-stuck. The actor only had to kick it as part of his tumble and it added to the tension and expectation that he was about to fall. When Craze clicks his fingers a member of stage crew quickly winches up the steel-wire line, and the actor is smoothly and speedily deposited at the top of the roof again. In the relief that ensues, he unclips the ring and makes his way down the attic hatch, usually to a burst of applause.

The actor's wedding suit required adjustment to cope with the harness, and also had to be dirtied in order that there was an appreciable difference to how it looked in Act 1. To achieve the latter the wardrobe department supplied two suits, complete with shirts. The actor could then appear suitably dressed in Act 1 for the wedding and dishevelled in Act 2. This switch, made during the interval, helped to illustrate the passage of time, as well as adding a touch of authenticity to the events as they unfolded.

Betty first appears in a smart suit, ready for her son's wedding. Later she puts on a fifties dance dress and a pair of flat-heeled pumps. The shoes enhanced the fifties style of the costume, but, more importantly, their non-slip soles aided the actor's walk onto the roof. In order to give her some extra support, some sash cord was put down one side of the chimney. This was painted and pinned to look like the cable from the television aerial, and was somewhat reassuring to an actor who suffered from vertigo, as she had to spend much of Act 2 sitting on the slope of the roof. The large chimney was also useful for Craze to hide behind and appear and disappear with apparent ease.

This production was difficult to light because it needed to be realistically the same light no matter where the set turned. As such, the lighting plan includes a repetition of **key light** (what the audience believes to be the main source of light) in various parts of the auditorium to cheat this idea.

Betty meets with the ghost of her dead lover and they dance together as they did in the fifties – a surreal encounter and lighted as such, creating a highly theatrical moment in the play. This was achieved by concealing lights within the set of the attic; for example, rope light was concealed in some plastic partition curtain. Lino lights, similar to the thin lights you may have in cupboards or bookshelves, were put in the attic floor joists, the lamp-shades in the tea-chests used for set dressing were wired up with bulbs so that they could flash, and birdie lights, which are small architectural fittings were concealed in the roof beams and spotlit the dance. Betty is transported into her past by listening to an old record. The record player had been wired to operate the turntable, but also had a light concealed within the front panel which lit her from the side as her memory takes hold. This prop provides a good illustration of the collaborative nature of theatre and the communication needed to take place between the different departments of set, props, sound and light.

Originally we had three stop positions for the revolve but during the technical rehearsal we tried the movement through these turns as one continuous journey, turning slowly rather than having three stops. The hatch position two was therefore not used. This kind of experimentation and deviation from the script is what technical rehearsals can be about. The exploration of scenic movement and the appropriateness to the action on stage may not necessarily result in an end product which reflects the writer's original intention.

At some point in a production, and *A Passionate Woman* was no exception, it is necessary to reach the top of a bar in its flown position, possibly to make adjustments to the level on the lines, or resetting effects, and certainly when positioning the angle of speakers and lights is required. To do this you will need access equipment, which is the generic term for any piece of equipment, which gets you off the floor. These are ladders, A-frames, tallescopes and cherry-pickers to name but a few. Here is a list of some types of access equipment; make yourself familiar with their names and their uses:

- **Access tower**: usually square or rectangular in section, built up from simple compo nents of scaffold pipes which clip together. They offer a large working area, but should always be climbed from the inside.
- **Tallescope**: the most common piece of access equipment used in theatre buildings. It may look and feel unstable, but it is very safe. There should be outriggers extended on it at all times and two people to manoeuvre it into position. The scope should never be pulled against the direction of the ladder, as this could tip it over.
- **Ladders**: some roof positions can only be reached from ladders. Great care should be exercised when a ladder is propped over a bar or pipe and, of course, this should never be done if the bars are attached to the flying system. In a fixed grid, where the scaffold pipes are attached to the walls, great care must be taken to ensure that the top of the ladder does not creep sideways as it is climbed. Two rungs protruding over the bar is considered safe. The bottom of a ladder should always be footed by a member of the team, standing with feet flat on the floor and holding the ladder to prevent any movement from left to right.
- **Zarges**: this structure is a combination of a straight ladder and an A-frame ladder. It is very stable and can reach difficult areas of the stage. It should also be used with someone footing the bottom of the ladder.

A Passionate Woman was commissioned for West Yorkshire Playhouse. There is some expectation then that it will work in a repertory theatre. However, repertory theatres are not all similar in design; whilst they may have similar resources and departments, the nature of each stage and its relationship to the audience is different.

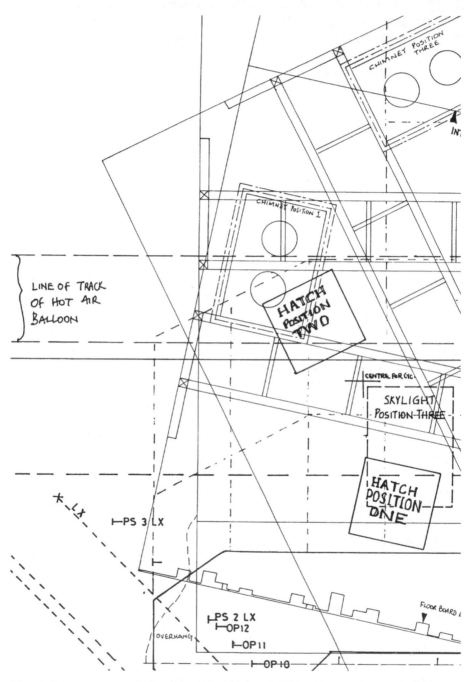

Figure 2.2 A section of the Haymarket Theatre, Leicester, with the ground plan of *A Passionate Woman* showing the changing positions of the revolve as it moved over hatch two.

Staffing Structures

The repertory theatre is based on the theatre as plant and machinery; it requires a theatre building in which performances and productions are made. It may be a privately funded theatre or a subsidised theatre. In the 1960s and 1970s theatre buildings in Britain were developed to produce particular types of work. They very often had two performance spaces – the main auditorium and a studio space. The latter was generally expected to be where the more experimental work was to be performed to a small and intimate audience. Studio spaces were highly flexible, allowing the seating to be placed in different arrangements and requiring significantly less scenery. The idea for the main theatre space was that it should provide a space which could play to a large audience both classic texts and contemporary plays. These two types of auditorium have determined the ways in which theatre progressed over the second half of the twentieth century.

The specialist departments needed to maintain and produce theatre tend to be large and the wide range of equipment in repertory theatre buildings is accepted as necessary for modern theatre production. These theatres were originally producing houses with full-time companies of actors and technicians. Although this arrangement is less common today, most repertory theatres have main auditoriums with flying systems of a counterweight nature; often in the larger national theatres these have computerised controls. The bars that are flown on the counterweights above the stage can carry scenery or lights. The stage itself can usually accommodate traps, which may be counterweighted or hydraulic. There is a prompt corner desk, from which shows can be cued by the deputy stage manager (DSM).

The openings of a stage to the auditorium vary from proscenium arch through to open thrust stages. In most cases, masking can be used to alter the shape and size of a proscenium opening. The amount of masking needed is determined by the sightlines; if an actor is in the wings and can see the audience, then it is safe to say that the audience can see the actor. Similarly, if you place a piece of set to the extreme left or right of the stage there will be a point at which members of the audience occupying the side seats of an auditorium cannot see that piece of set. A recognition of this is most important, as it indicates areas of the stage which are 'dead'. It also suggests the need for masking into the wings, in order to conceal theatrical mechanisms from the audience. The argument for better sightlines was first put forward by Francesco Algarotti (1712–64) in *An Essay on the Opera* (1755); a connoisseur of the arts and sciences, he advocated a greater concentration on the stage picture and masking was to enable this focus. In the nineteenth century the German composer Richard Wagner (1813–83) demanded the removal of all distractions inherent in the tiered auditorium, and he got his wish with the building of the Festspielhaus at Bayreuth, which was constructed at very little expense, partly because it was a summer theatre and required no heating. The most important design feature of this theatre was the fan-shaped auditorium, thought to be a more democratic seating arrangement for the audience as it enabled the same view of the stage scene for every audience member. This arrangement is similar to cinema architecture and has become less appropriate for live performance which is non-naturalistic in style and does not require the use of the box set; that is, a set which represents a room with side walls.

So far in this section we have looked at the method of making a simple structure like a flat, how these structures form the basis of scenic construction and how scenic pieces are moved and flown. Scenic elements, by their nature, are often specifically built pieces designed for a single production or even a single performance. However, there are standard pieces and features which some venues have as stock units. The most common of these and the ones that directly offer a framing facility are the masking features. As we have seen, in a proscenium arch stage the masking is fairly straightforward as it simply blocks angles of vision into the wings and into the fly tower from the front rows of the auditorium. Masking becomes more complicated when scenic features are required to fly in and be lit, and even more difficult as the space between objects and bars becomes more limited. The decisions about masking are usually taken by the whole design team and the Production Manager and there should be an attempt to create a harmonious look for the work.

If you wish to create an illusion and an element of surprise, then it is most important that the audience cannot see either people or objects before those objects enter the stage space. The masking can be curtains (**soft masking**) or black flats with plywood fronts (**hard masking**). (Because of its colour most masking is referred to collectively as **blacks**.) Soft masking can be tied to a bar using a simple bow and so is quick to put up and easy to get into tight corners. **Ballet masking** sits parallel to the front of the stage and goes off into the wings. It allows actors or dancers to make their entrance easily without the audience being aware of the point of entry on to the stage. Ballet masking is sometimes created using **legs**, narrow lengths of drape that hang vertically from a bar. In order to conceal from view lighting bars or other pieces of the flying mechanisms, shallow lengths of drape, known as **borders**, hang horizontally. When soft masking is not in use it should be folded away and stored in a dry place.

Jobs in a Repertory Theatre

The number of personnel in each department will depend on the size of the theatre and its budget. The roles listed here are those which can comfortably manage to produce shows within a theatre building. The most common turnaround for the staging of productions is something in the region of three to five weeks. This means that all staff will be running a public performance six nights a week, whilst in rehearsal for the next production, and very often planning the subsequent one. The need for very clear systems of communication is paramount in order for this amount of work to be completed successfully.

Stage Management
The team – Company Stage Manager, Deputy Stage Manager, Assistant Stage Manager

The stage management team is responsible for the smooth running of communications and acts as the conduit for each of the departments. The Company Stage Manager (CSM) not only oversees these communications during ongoing productions but also co-ordinates personnel for the preparation of other shows in rehearsal. This person has his or her finger on the pulse of the whole technical team. The Deputy Stage Manager (DSM) will be in rehearsal each day for the next production and in the evening may cue the show in performance. The Assistant Stage Manager (ASM) will perform tasks for the show in rehearsal during the day and maintain props for the evening's performance, and is involved in scene changes, costume changes, or perhaps even cooking a meal to be eaten on stage should the play require it.

The CSM, then, is at any one time responsible for two companies of actors. One which is performing and one which is in rehearsal. They collate lists of the actors' accommodation details in order that they may be contacted on a daily basis. In addition, the CSM often chairs meetings and reports to the appropriate departments details which are relevant to each production. They co-ordinate meetings with the theatre's technical staff and any contracted staff, who are usually designers and directors.

Once the production has begun rehearsal, this role is taken on by the DSM, who becomes the conduit between the rehearsal room and the theatre building. Sometimes rehearsals take place away from the theatre itself, but even when this is not the case, because of the amount of work going on in the theatre, notes from rehearsal are written out every day. These contain information and requests to the relevant departments. It is this flow of communication that enables technicians to engage with the variety of problems which arise in a particular production. Rehearsal is a continual process of research and development and so each note is numbered and dated to provide an up-to-date record of production requirements.

The ASM often has the responsibility for props and will work closely with the designer to acquire the appropriate items. This liaison is most important with contracted designers, who may be unfamiliar with the town in which they find themselves working. ASMs must research the period and have a clear understanding of the props needed for the production. They also check the theatre's own store for suitable properties, and liaise with departments which may have to alter objects after they have been purchased. They occasionally contact business companies and members of the general public to find objects which may be loaned or given to the theatre, and are responsible for making arrangements for the collection and return of props once the run of the show is over. The ASM often works during each performance and can report to the DSM when repairs of set, props or costume are required throughout the run of the show. The DSM notes these items in the **show report**, which must be written up after each performance.

Workshop Construction and Stage Mechanisms
The Team – Master Carpenter, Deputy Carpenter, Scenic Artist, Prop-maker, Technical Stage Manager, Head Flyman, Stage Technician, Stage Crew

The overlap of the jobs between these personnel will depend on the size of theatre and its budget. It will also depend on the nature of productions undertaken by the theatre. All these people have a responsibility for the completion of scenery, its use on stage and the smooth running of any mechanisms required by the production. Very often their skills are not strictly delineated; however, there is usually one person responsible for the safe working of the stage floor and the safe working of all flying components.

Designer's Model Box

A scale model made from card, wood, cloth or any other materials which will convey a sense of the world to be created on the stage. All departments refer to the model, which provides important insights into the ways in which solutions to technical problems can be discovered. Any structures which are to appear on stage must be contained within the model.

It is important to note that although some theatre design exhibits contain quite perfect models, the model is a working tool whose function is to convey the intention of the design team and director. It is not an art object in its own right, but an expression of the work in progress and the work still to be carried out. The model is therefore vital for the scenic artist as a reference for colour and texture.

The Master Carpenter and the Deputy Master Carpenter manage a team of workers who liaise with the designer on the construction of the stage set. The designer's **model box** of the set, together with his or her drawings, are redrawn and discussed by the carpenters and designers in order to produce the desired effect within the budget allocated. Working with the scenic artist, the carpenters create these effects by employing certain techniques to make a piece of scenery seem more solid than it actually is, or paint a grain or stone effect, which is obviously cheaper than constructing the set with real materials. The appropriateness of these techniques will depend on the overall aesthetic aspiration of the production, which will have been established by the design team and the director.

The Technical Stage Manager co-ordinates the technology on stage and will be the person who solves technical problems with any of the stage mechanisms. He or she will be responsible for instructing the stage crew as to the operation of equipment during the production. The Technical Manager receives information from the DSM and liaises with the flyman and Production Manager as to how particular changes might be achieved. This person needs a sound understanding of how people and three-dimensional objects can be moved about the stage, and is also responsible for safe working practices on the stage.

The flyman works with the DSM and Technical Manager, and is skilled in operating single- and double-purchase counterweight systems, winches, and motors, and, if appropriate, computerised flying systems. The flyman is also responsible for the safe working and maintenance of these systems. He loads and balances the weight of flown objects with weights which are placed in a **cradle**. The flyman is thus able to move objects which would normally be beyond his physical strength. He is also responsible for the correct balancing of the bars that contain lights and scenic features. Some theatres employ hydraulic operators and have an engineering department.

Electrics and Lighting
The Team – Chief Electrician, Deputy Chief Electrician, Assistant Electrician

The Chief Electrician (also known as Head of Lighting) is responsible for the management of lighting in all its aspects. In theatres which do not have a dedicated sound department the Chief Electrician will undertake the management of this area as well, and occasionally the lighting design for some productions. His or her main role, however, is to respond to the requests of the freelance lighting designer, who is usually engaged for each production, and to liaise with the design team and director to create the desired lighting aesthetic. The lighting designer supplies a series of plans for the stage lighting, which indicate symbols of the specific units to be used. In addition, the electrics department will undertake the making of practical props should they require illumination and also the use of special effects such as pyrotechnics and smoke. The Chief Electrician and the deputy work together to achieve the completion of all this work and the general maintenance of equipment and computer systems for the operation of lights. Once they have the plans from the lighting designer they are able to ensure that any problems caused by masking or set changes can be eradicated. The Chief Electrician is responsible for negotiating the necessary stage time in order to facilitate the rigging, focusing and plotting of the lighting changes, all within the budget set by the Production Manager.

The Assistant Electrician will often be involved in the preparation of practical props and the day-to-day maintenance of the lighting department, and, prior to the production week, will be preparing all the extra pieces of equipment necessary for the production. During the run, he or she will be involved with the rest of the team in rigging and focusing the lights.

Sound
The Team – Head of Sound, Deputy Head of Sound, Assistant Sound Technician

These jobs will depend on the size of the theatre and therefore the size of the sound department. The Head of Sound is responsible for the making of a **sound plot**, which facilitates the desired effects for the production, and may be recorded on to a variety of playback formats. This member of staff will work to accommodate the ideas of a sound designer, if one has been contracted. In general, the Head of Sound liaises with the DSM, sound designer and director for the particular requirements of each production. The Assistant Electrician will help in the sound department, in terms of maintenance and operation of equipment.

Wardrobe
The Team – Wardrobe Supervisor, Deputy Wardrobe Manager, Wardrobe Assistant

The Wardrobe Supervisor runs the wardrobe department and is responsible for providing designers with the costumes they have designed. The supervisor negotiates with the designer which costumes can come from the theatre's costume store, which may need alteration, which can be bought, and which need to be made. The supervisor is usually highly skilled at cutting and making, has a comprehensive knowledge of periods and styles, and can replicate a style using the fastest and most authentic-looking means. A vast knowledge of materials and textures, appropriate for different historical and modern fabrics, is essential. The supervisor also manages the washing and maintenance of costumes used in performance and, with the deputy and assistant, manage any quick changes during the run of the production. In some wardrobe departments the supervisor and deputy wardrobe manager will alternate responsibility for shows, in order that one may be planning the next production requirements, while the other is in production week. The Wardrobe Supervisor is responsible for engaging makers and any other relevant staff to complete the costumes and must keep within the budget.

Production Management
The Team – Production Manager, Production Assistant

The Production Manager oversees the production through the technical departments and the requirements of the **scenographic team**; the latter is usually contracted per production to design the overall visual and aural elements of a production. The job of Production Manager is a balancing act: he or she must provide, where possible and with the assistance of the technical departments, all that is requested, while shouldering the responsibility for keeping the production costs of materials and technical personnel within the budget. The budget is often set by the Chief Executive of the theatre, who may be an administrator or an artistic director. The production budget is only a partial costing of the production, as it does not include actors' wages, administration, marketing and publicity. The Production Manager must therefore make an assessment of the production cost to each department, based on the aesthetic choices made by the scenographic team. An initial production meeting is called to discuss the designer's model and the way in which certain aspects of the production may be achieved. At this meeting the Production Manager allocates a budget to each department. The departments must then assess whether they can work within the sum allowed and it may be necessary for the Production Manager to adjust the figures in order to accommodate the designs. One key principle of production management is always to keep some contingency finance in reserve, which can be used to solve unforeseen problems. The budget for *A Passionate Woman* was:

Set	£6,000
Props	£500
Costumes	£2,000
Wardrobe travel	£200
Lighting	£700
Sound	£250
Stage management props	£500
Paint	£500
Total budget	£10,650

The Production Manager is responsible for the production up to the moment of the first

Health & Safety

Many items of equipment, which are needed to carry out work above the stage floor, will either have to be hauled up access equipment, or put on the end of a rope and pulled up. Always ensure that you are secure and never carry a very heavy object up a steep ladder if you do not have both hands free. It is much easier first to climb up with a coil of rope and drop this down for your team to tie onto any equipment you may need. Avoid lifting equipment above anyone's head, including your own. Hard hats must be worn when people are working overhead. If you do drop something from above, the warning HEADS! should be given. You must also give the warning if you are intentionally about to drop something to the stage floor, like a cloth, for instance. Wait until the warning has been heeded before you carry on and shout it the moment you drop anything.

performance. Once this has been achieved, he or she is usually well ensconced in the next production: as with all the staff in a producing house, the Production Manager is planning for one production, while seeing another into completion, and preparing meetings with designers and suggesting budgets which may finance future productions. In some theatre buildings there will be a Production Assistant to help co-ordinate the staff of the various departments and the contracted design or scenographic teams.

As an example, here is a list of job titles in Nottingham Playhouse.

Production Manager
Production Assistant
Technical Manager
Stage Technician
Stage Manager (2)
Deputy Stage Manager (2)
Assistant Stage Manager (?)
Head of Construction
Deputy Construction Manager
Carpenter
Chief Electrician
Deputy Chief Electrician Lighting
Deputy Chief Electrician Sound
Assistant Electrician
Head of Props
Deputy of Head of Props
Head of Paintshop
Deputy Head of Paintshop

These are just some of the jobs that are available in building-based theatres which produce their own work and which also may receive work from touring companies. The amount of staff in each department will depend on the number of theatre spaces that are contained within the building.

In this chapter we have looked at the staffing structures and at some of the scenic mechanisms used in a theatre building to create illusion. The key idea behind this kind of technical theatre is that the illusion created is coherent with the story being told.

Staging Shakespeare

The Text

One of the distinctive features of Shakespeare and something that is frequently commented upon is the relevance of his themes to contemporary society. Productions of Shakespeare's work can therefore be quite free in their interpretation of the place and time of the action. It is this level of interpretation that inevitably leads to a conceptual understanding of the play. Nona Shepphard's interpretation of *Romeo and Juliet* set the drama in the early seventeenth century – roughly the period in which Shakespeare was writing – but changed the location from Italy to India, just at a time when British merchants were starting to gain a foothold in their quest for spice and silk. The feud in this interpretation, then, is between the Montagues, a family of London merchants, and the Capulets, a family of Indian merchants – Lord Capulet being one of the richest traders in the area, with a daughter whose marriage has been arranged to a local nobleman. The Montagues are a Catholic family escaping Protestant persecution at home, and bring with them a missionary, Friar Lawrence. The feud between the families centres around trading rivalries, and is underscored by racism and fear of immigration; Friar Lawrence's desire to win converts to the Catholic faith becomes an added factor in his meddling, which inadvertently causes the tragedy. These issues are relevant to contemporary society and Shepphard's concept presented some interesting opportunities for research and execution in design.

Technical Challenges

The immediacy of the text is brought to life through the production. The designer translated this into an open stage space, hung on all sides with muslin, which created a kind of tented space. A number of ropes placed about the stage and hung from the flys were mainly decorative, but one was used for the murder of Tybalt, when Romeo puts an end to his life after the sword fight by strangling him, and leaves him hanging. On the stage there needed to be an indication of the street; the house of the Capulets, including the ballroom and Juliet's bedroom; the Friar's cell and the Capulet tomb. In addition, the play goes from Verona to Mantua and back, but only for brief moments. And of course there is a need for a balcony.

The floor of this open space, painted to shade from cream to a deep ochre, had a centre triangle from front to back, made of canvas and suggesting a central road running into the distance. The designer created a beautiful colonnaded Mogul tower, made as a **truck**, the top of which was Juliet's bedroom and balcony, and the bottom became part of the house furnished with carpets and furniture. This castored platform was moved on and off stage by means of a winch line. The ballroom was created by three long drops of blue silk which tumbled in from the flys. Friar Lawrence's cell also flew in and was a muslin tent, weighted with stones and hung with drying herbs. The Capulet tomb was created by two huge mask-like figures suggesting protective deities, which were carried on by two ASMs, Juliet having been carried on by the cast in procession, and covered with flowers to suggest a Hindu funeral.

The action in many of Shakespeare's plays is fast and *Romeo and Juliet* has a complex plot, which moves at a brisk pace. The open stage space for this production allowed this dynamic to maintain the pace and avoid laborious scene changes. It is worth considering this with your own work. Scene changes can act as punctuation, offer the audience a moment for reflection and release from tension, but conversely it may be necessary to maintain the tension of the drama, which a scene change would disrupt. This then becomes a design and technical decision and has much to do with your idea of how to approach the work.

Health & Safety

Naked flames and inherently fire-proof materials: some theatres, due to their fire regulations, cannot use naked flames on stage (i.e. candles or torches). In order to create a torch light effect, we first had to design the fitting which the artificial flame would sit in. We then used a commercial lighting technique which used a 12 V fan with a 12 V dichroic bulb; this was wired to a sealed unit 12 V battery. Car batteries cannot be used on stage, as they can give off fumes and are potentially flammable. The sealed lead acid battery could be hidden in the base of the torch which could be carried on and off stage at different points in the action. Electricity is discussed in Chapter 7.

The first challenge in this production was the budget. The original plan had been to surround the stage area with white muslin and the floor cloth would then have extended off into the wings. There would be no black masking and the actors would be on view from the moment they entered the space. The cost of such an amount of material was prohibitive, however, so the muslin was brought into the confines of the normal stage space. This meant that the material ran across the back of the stage and up and down both sides. The truck had to be concealed until it was needed, and had to be able to travel at a steady pace with no stage management or actors pushing it. There was a lot of flying, as the designer felt it was the quickest and sometimes most spectacular way to transform this empty space. And it is true that this is one of the most magical features of technical theatre.

The enclosed environment of muslin meant that there were only overhead positions for lighting and positions from the front. The team decided that torches would enhance the atmosphere and add to the sense of the period. However, due to Health & Safety rulings, candles or naked flames on stage were not permitted, so an alternative method was called for.

Costumes

The director had a cast of twelve actors, which, for a professional production, is quite a large company. However, there were in all twenty-four parts, if the musicians and servants of the household are included. In order to people the stage, Sheppard decided that she would use face masks, and in two distinct ways. First, the servants, musicians, Friar Lawrence, and the men who fight in the opening scene were masked. The masks were striking and the designer researched a variety of sources for these references. She found contemporary paintings of the British in India sporting doublets, ruffs and velvets, despite the hot climate. The idea was that the set should be hung with the cotton and silks and decorated with huge bowls of spices, much sought after in Europe. The two sets of costumes were in different colour dyes – the spice dyes of India and the root dyes of Europe – and reflected the differing textures and styles of dress worn by

Figure 3.1 A scene from *Romeo and Juliet* at Leicester Haymarket Theatre showing the Mogul tower and Juliet's balcony.

Figure 3.2 A scene from *Romeo and Juliet*: the Capulets' ball. Note the costumes and masks, as well as the silk drapes and muslin cyclorama.

the Indian characters and the Europeans. She also researched Indian masks and the masks of the commedia dell'arte. These masks dictated a comic approach which the director felt was true to the text, and needed to be brought out to throw the tragedy into relief. The masks used in the masked ball were more formal, often on sticks and bejewelled, beribboned and very colourful. On such a set, costume design was a major feature. The Indian clothes were made of silk of all kinds, from rough to fine, with muslin and cotton also featuring. The Elizabethans were dressed in velvets, brocades, chenille, satins, leather, suede and cotton. The contrast between Lady Capulet, graceful in flowing deep blue and purple silks, with flashing golden bangles and sparkling jewels in her black hair which fell in a plait to her waist and tiny silk slippers on her feet, and Lady Montague, striding around in a rust-coloured velvet bodices and brocaded flounced skirt, a jaunty suede hat sporting a feather, pearl drops in her ears, and boots on her feet, gives the clearest picture of the characters of these two women and the two distinct cultures living in the same town.

In the preparation for costuming a production, the designer starts by reading the text and developing lists of ideas of what is needed in terms of action and taking into account those aspects which are pertinent to plot and subtext that need to be conveyed through costume. Costumes must be appropriate for the characters and consultation with the actors is beneficial. The designer's job is to help develop environment and atmospheres which are true to the emotional and physical space in which these characters interact. The costume can be almost a living partner to the performer. In the first years of the Theatre Laboratory, Jerzy Grotowski (1933–99) referred to such costume as a prosthesis which assists the performer, continuously transforming their shape and energy: in other words the costume itself performs.

The costume design is often, but not necessarily, completed by the person who designs the set. What is necessary is communication between the theatre workers in these and related areas: an appropriate synergy of ideas about the text and production, leading to choices for the set and the costumes which are complementary. For example, it is not helpful for a beige set to have performers in beige costumes, for obvious reasons. It is worth bearing in mind not only what the individual will look like in the colours and textures in which they are dressed but also what they will look like against the environment which is created.

We all show aspects of our character through the clothes we wear and we tend to judge people we meet for the first time by their appearance. The importance of costumes to the presentation of the performance, therefore, cannot be emphasised too strongly. Costumes can help define character. The characters of most plays are rarely two dimensional and so costume needs to be sophisticated and effective. It enables the audience to understand conventions and manners of the time. In Shepphard's production of *Romeo and Juliet*, for example, the colour of Lord Capulet's costume was a very distinctive green, which had been taken from the paintings of the time, and members of his household wore turbans of that colour. Ultimately, costumes should work to preserve the unity of the production.

Many period costumes are difficult to wear. For example, a Victorian evening dress would have been worn with a corset and Victorian women of a particular class were very proud of their slim waistlines. A designer of such a costume may expect an actress to wear a corset but could hardly insist on an eighteen-inch waist. The trick here would be to exaggerate the detail at the shoulders and hips to make the waistline appear narrow, while allowing the actress to breathe and move comfortably. If a costume has become a significant element in the overall design, it is important that the performer has plenty of time in rehearsal to try on and use the costume so that it can be adjusted for her or his ease of movement.

Costumes for a production can be made in-house, or the job can be sent out to makers, or they can be bought or hired. It would be rare for costumes, other than those hired, to be taken 'off the peg' without some adaptation or embellishment, a fact that should be borne in mind in terms of budget and time. Costumes made in-house must be made to measure for the actors and patterns are therefore cut for each costume. The costumes are then sewn, fitted and decorated. Jumble sales and second-hand shops are good places to find particular items of clothing or fabric and often a theatre company can use and re-use costumes from stock. The wardrobe department is also responsible for wigs, hairstyles and accessories. Footwear must also reflect the correct period and make dance or vigorous movement possible. If all these features are considered with care you will present a performer evocatively dressed for the character he or she is playing.

In designing costumes for Oscar Wilde's *The Importance of Being Earnest* (1895), a starting point will be an investigation into the costumes of the period. Differences in ages and levels of sophistication between the female characters can be subtly indicated through the dresses they wear. In Act 2 the text requires that Jack should wear formal mourning dress and that Dr Chasuble should wear the correct clerical dress. All these aspects must be researched and designed, taking into account the interpretation and the style and colours to be used in the set. In addition, a character may require more than one costume during the play, which has four acts. The question should be asked, Does each character require different costumes for each act? What time has passed from act to act?

Would Gwendolen visit the country in her town clothes? Costume is a sure way of suggesting mood and the passing of time.

When do these costume changes occur and how long does an actor have to change? **Quick changes** are those which occur while the play is in performance. If a quick change is necessary, the designer must design costumes which can easily be put on and taken off. A costume may need to be changed on stage or have pieces added to it and this must also be designed to ensure the changes can be made without fumbling and as a continuation of the action. Ideally, such costumes must be fitted well in advance, so that the actor can practise with them before the **technical rehearsal**, when the technical changes which occur in the production are rehearsed. On a proscenium arch stage it is possible to cheat if the audience is at a distance from the performer, but in the round or on a thrust stage, or where the audience is close to the action, the fastenings of costume must be appropriate. For example, medieval costumes must be laced rather than zipped, and decorations must be sewn rather than fixed with Velcro, if a sense of authenticity is to be maintained. There are, of course, various tricks to help achieve these changes. In quick changes that involve shirts or other buttoned items of clothing a short piece of elastic can be sewn to buttons so that the fastenings can be swiftly pulled open. Elastic can be added to laced-up shoes, so that they slip on and off easily.

Emblems and Symbols

While symbolism in theatre is as old as theatre itself, in the late nineteenth century a Symbolist movement began in France. The movement viewed the theatre not only as a means of expression but also a means of understanding the world. They wished the theatre to reflect mental and spiritual life rather than just appeal to the senses. The major poet and thinker in this movement was Stéphane Mallarmé (1842–98), who believed art was a mode of acquiring knowledge, perception, intuition and reasoning. Playwrights of this genre are the French actor-manager André Antoine (1858–1943) and the Belgian dramatist Maurice Maeterlinck (1862–1949). Sometimes cited as the precursor of absurdism, Maeterlinck was fascinated by the mysterious forces that make life elusive. His *Pelléas et Mélisande* (1892) inspired Claude Debussy's opera of 1902, and *L'Oiseau blue* was first produced by Stanislavsky and performed by the Moscow Art Theatre in 1908.

Symbolism is discussed in Chapter 5.

Making a disguise – Masks

In medieval drama, emblems and symbols figured strongly. In the Tudor period, disguise was used and the switching of costumes made for very dramatic moments, as well as helping a performer play more than one part. As we have seen, the characteristic doubling of parts in an Elizabethan play has a bearing on decisions about costume. The mask's function is to make the performer abstract and change them in character fundamentally.

The masks for *Romeo and Juliet* were made from casts of the actors' faces. They were lined with soft material and given a skin tone which indicated which household they belonged to. They were attached to the head with elastic or ribbon.

Elizabethan Theatre Space

The space in which a piece of theatre is to be performed has a crucial effect on the interpretation of the performance. Shakespeare, along with the actors which formed the Globe Company, specifically chose the design and features of the Globe Theatre – the space in which many of his plays were performed. The first Globe theatre of 1599 was designed by actors and based on their experience of the best architectural arrangement for the kinds of plays they performed. The choices they made, in terms of architectural features, informed their performance style and the pace of the production. They also determined the type of presentation which was most suitable for this theatre building and the scenographic elements bore a direct relation to that space. The Globe worked as a commercial space, regularly producing new plays. In this respect it is likely that the plays would have been required to almost direct themselves around the space due to the shortage of time for rehearsal and other commercial pressures. (Shakespeare's company was, however, latterly supported by a patron.)

The Elizabethan stage had particular features and staging areas. When James Burbage (*c.* 1530–97) undertook to build a theatre in London in 1576, he had three sources from which to draw ideas:

1 the known features, which had been effective for theatrical presentation for hundreds of years;
2 the structural elements in public and private buildings, in which actors had performed up until this time. His combination of 1 and 2 served as a model for all those theatres built in London over the next eighty-seven years – a model which in turn has influenced plans of theatres today;
3 the work of John Brayne, Burbage's brother-in-law, who had built the Red Lion Theatre in Stepney, London. Brayne had engaged a carpenter, William Sylvester, to make theatrical provisions at the Red Lion. A lawsuit was brought against Brayne in 1569 because he failed to pay for the structure when it was completed. It is from the record of the case that we discover most of our information about the Red Lion. The documents indicate that there was a new and independent structure, an amphitheatre. The stage, its turret and surrounding galleries suggest that Brayne knew what he wanted, regardless of cost.

All the features of the Red Lion are consistent with what came later in the Boar's Head Theatre, 1602, and the Globe Theatre, 1599. Brayne brought his experience of building the Red Lion to the construction of The Theatre in Shoreditch, the first purpose-built theatre in London, where he worked with James Burbage. In 1599 a syndicate, which included Shakespeare, was formed to build the Globe. As the syndicate was financing the project, it is safe to assume that the Globe stage met all the requirements of Shakespeare and his companions. With the exception of Cuthbert Burbage, James's son, all members of the syndicate were actors. This meant that the construction of the acting areas could be supervised by those who would use them, an opportunity rarely afforded to actors in modern British theatre. Until 1599, Shakespeare had written plays for the type of stages found in the inn yards, The Theatre and possibly The Curtain, which was London's second purpose-built playhouse. When The Theatre's ground lease ran out it was dismantled and its timbers were used in the construction of the first Globe Theatre. Once the Globe had been built, Shakespeare could take advantage of more efficient and effective means of production and more elaborate staging, both for new plays and for the revival of old ones.

Without doubt, Burbage and Brayne were influenced by classical theatre and chose an amphitheatrical shape for the space allocated to the audience, similar to that in bear-baiting rings, common at that time on the south bank of the Thames. Brayne's Red Lion, however, did not resemble a bear ring or a Tudor hall and the architectural features of The Theatre were not merely functional – both men understood the potential in architecture to support drama. The essential device of the playhouse lay in its geometric plan and the design was all of one piece, a complete unit whose timbers slotted together. This construction allowed it to be erected in a very short time. Burbage and Brayne were also concerned with audience capacity, **acoustics**, or the way sound behaves within a given space, sightlines and provision for the needs of the players.

The second Globe Theatre of 1614 had an enormous roof over the stage, sometimes referred to as the **heavens**, which contained mechanisms for flying objects and for creating sound effects, as recorded in the engraving by Wenceslaus Hollar (1607–77). It is thought that the underside was painted with stars and signs of the zodiac. The heavens were not an original feature of the Elizabethan playhouse as conceived by Burbage and Brayne. At the Red Lion the large stage was surmounted by a tall timber turret, capable of supporting a simple flying machine, and the stage was left uncovered. In this respect, the mechanics of the stage were similar to that of the classical theatre and to the kinds of operations undertaken on medieval wagons. The actors had used a stage door in order to separate themselves from the paying audience at the Red Lion. Thus two doors, one for the actors, one for the audience, were maintained in the 1599 Globe building. Burbage copied the bear ring arrangement of three levels for the seating. Within the galleries were tiers of benches, with standing room at the highest level at the back; partitions of varying heights divided the tiers into sections.

The yard area was most probably raked, allowing water drainage and also better visibility for those seated in the first level of the gallery. Stage directions in Shakespeare's plays suggest there may have been up to five traps in the stage: a small one at each of the four corners, capable of carrying one person, and a long narrow one across the centre which could bear as many as eight people, including elaborate and heavy props. As the traps were very noisy to operate, there is often a stage direction or text implication for music, thunder, blasts on wind instruments or a drum roll. The music would have been played in the musicians' gallery, which, being housed in the third tier above the stage, would have been rarely required as an acting space or audience seating area. The sound effects of thunder and of battles would have been operated in the **huts**, which were located above the canopy of the stage. Inside the huts were mechanisms for flying illusions; it is conceivable that actors would have been flown for certain roles, perhaps the fairies in *A Midsummer Night's Dream* and Ariel in *The Tempest*.

The stage was backed and roofed, which allowed for entrance and exit doors and protection from inclement weather. The carved screen of the Great Hall of a wealthy patron, with its two doors at the side, formed the architectural source of the rear façade. These doors have ceased to be of practical use in modern times and now flank the proscenium arch stage, or are simply decorative devices in the proscenium itself, as in the Royal

Shakespeare Theatre at Stratford-upon-Avon, the Theatre Royal, Bury St Edmunds, and the Richmond Theatre, Yorkshire. The Globe's façade resembled a three-storey Elizabethan house, topped by a gabled attic rising above the roof and the third gallery. In the centre of the façade was a curtained alcove which formed an inner stage, which had a door to the **stage left** and a window in the back wall to the **stage right**. (Stage left and stage right refers to the positions when standing on stage facing the audience.) The door could open and reveal the foot of the staircase leading to the second storey, which also had a curtained alcove in the centre. These alcoves resemble the modern box set, but instead of solid walls the Elizabethan set had curtains.

There are three ways in which the alcove could be used: (1) as an interior in its own right; (2) as an extension of an interior scene, signified by placing set or objects further downstage, such as a throne, or a bed; or (3) as a backing to a scene played further downstage with the curtains closed, or used as an arras, as required in the text of *Hamlet*, to conceal Polonius in Gertrude's bedchamber. In the floor of the inner stage was a long narrow trap door, known as the **grave**, which could be used for ghostly apparitions or for descents to a vault or underground prison. In *Hamlet* it would have been used for the burial of Ophelia and the grave-diggers' scene.

The timbers used in the construction of the Globe determined the octagonal shape of the theatre. This shape offered two other areas for acting – window bays, which appeared separate from the stage area and were supported by slender columns and resembled the kind of architectural features found in a Tudor domestic dwelling.

All these features offered different levels, platforms, spaces and balconies on which to perform the scenes. The variety of settings afforded quick changes in location from scene to scene with little formal scenery changing. Often scenes could be played simultaneously or at least overlap to form a seamless picture of the life and ideas presented. This overlapping would have considerably cut the length of the plays. It also meant that the audience could tune in and out of the action and be led around the theatre as necessary – a promenade for the eye.

After 1599 Shakespeare was writing specifically for this stage. He did not need to write copious stage directions as he knew the space extremely well – not least because he often performed in his own plays. This lack of stage directions consequently allows for individual interpretation and frees the reader, performer and audience from preconceived notions of the location of the piece. It is this openness that allows Shakespeare's work to be played in such a multiplicity of settings for modern audiences. Modern interpretations of Shakespeare are often criticised for being visually cluttered. A search for clarity in the presentation of these plays has preoccupied many actors, actor-managers, producers, directors and designers.

Hamlet

The multistage setting of the Elizabethan theatre is something which modern theatre architects are often striving to re-create – a flexible performance space, suitable for the playing of any play. In *Hamlet* there is an almost continual sense of movement around the interior of the castle. We meet the characters wandering through the castle, but we are rarely told of the detail of the rooms. The design of a production relies on the individual producer, director and designer's approach to the play to guide the style or method of that production. The design is also influenced by the theatre spaces which have evolved for performance. For instance, a design could be utilitarian; that is, we are presented with a setting that offers a functional approach to the play. We could call Elizabethan staging a utilitarian set in the sense that the use of the actual theatre is the setting. The performance is uninterrupted by scene changes, which enables a fast moving piece of theatre, where the characters wander the corridors of Elsinore. The theatre building has doors which characters can pass in and out of, whilst plotting their next move. There are different levels from which characters can look out of the castle, perhaps across the battlements, and there are enclosed spaces for the more intimate scenes. The open stage provides us with a battlefield, and the grave trap provides a churchyard.

Western theatre has gone through many different styles and different staging, and different buildings have evolved. The design for *Hamlet* in London's Lyceum Theatre of 1864 differed from the Elizabethan approach. Charles Fechter (1824–79) played Hamlet and the action was performed in front of a series of beautifully painted backdrops, the majority of which was designed and executed by the artist William Telbin. The audience would have visited the theatre to see the sets as much as to see the play. Between each act the curtain would drop in order to allow the painted scene to be changed. Musical entertainment was provided by a band, which would strike up between each act. It played a variety of music to accompany this production of *Hamlet*, from Mozart's overture to *Don Giovanni* to Rossini's overture to *Guillaume Tell* after Act 3, and at the end of the play 'Vivi Tu', from Donizetti's *Anna Bolena*. This was spectacle theatre and actor-managers relied on gimmicks to attract audiences. By 1892, English actor-manager Herbert Beerbohm Tree (1853–1917) was performing *Hamlet*. During this period it was deemed essential that all theatrical settings should be historically accurate.

The recent invention and use of electric light in theatres highlighted the paintings, as opposed to the general murk of gaslight, in which they had previously been presented. William Telbin's painting for *Hamlet* at the Lyceum Theatre, though two-dimensional, had some features from the Elizabethan stage – for instance, a raised room at the back of the stage, where the Players could perform before the assembled court. Understandably, it was felt necessary to present this scene in a special space. So we have the effect of a play within a play quite literally echoed in the stage presentation. The upstage area is painted to give a very similar look to that of the Elizabethan inner alcove or inner stage, suggesting a room behind the action. The costumes are a Victorian interpretation of the period in which Hamlet is set, around the beginning of the thirteenth century.

In 1911, the English stage designer Gordon Craig (1872–1966) was asked to design a production of *Hamlet* for the Moscow Art Theatre. Craig's theory hinged on this principle: 'When producing great drama, I have never been concerned in any attempt to show the spectators an exact view of some historical period in architecture. I always feel that all great plays have an order of architecture which is more or less theatrical, unreal as the play' (Bablet, 1981:188). Craig had been an actor under Henry Irving (1838–1905) at the Lyceum Theatre and had seen the shortcomings of the gaslit, two-dimensional settings. He attended a scenic art lecture by Hubert von Herkomer in 1892, which questioned various features of the theatre of the day. Herkomer noted that the angle of viewing from the upper balconies of most theatres made the actors appear foreshortened; the footlights cast unnatural shadows on the actors' faces; the quality of the painted scenery was flat and lifeless. He demonstrated which atmospheric effects could be achieved by using electric lights, lantern slides and gauzes. Although the reasons for these experiments was to create spectacle, Craig saw their potential for a new style of theatrical presentation and in his production of *Hamlet* he used some of these features.

In Craig's collaboration with Stanislavsky (1865–1938), *Hamlet* was conceived as a monodrama in which the prince is the only real person, all others are a figment of his imagination. The innovative design for the production was a system of screens which moved into various positions about the stage. These were architectonic forms which moved in all directions at any speed to create endlessly variable scenic environments which could be coloured with electric light or decorated with projections. However, Craig was not an engineer and the screens did not move as easily as planned, and, consequently, were ill-suited to the scenic fluidity which *Hamlet* demands.

Craig did not want the traditional curtain between scenes; instead he wished the scene changes to be visible, hoping that sight of the scene setters would make the audience conscious of a symbolic performance. His approach involved the audience's awareness of the labour of theatre and, like Herkomer, Craig recognised that this was part of its magic. In the first few nights of performance the screens were so precarious that the curtains had to be drawn each time the set was changed. The screens were made of light wooden frames covered with grey transparent canvas and fitted with reversible hinges. Unfortunately they had a tendency to topple over and on the first night, in Moscow, it is said that they fell like dominoes. Craig's design concept, however, was a success and after the first night, as is often the case, the production settled in and adjustments were made. According to Stanislavsky, 'The production of *Hamlet* met with great success. Some people were enthusiastic, others criticised, but everybody was excited, and debated, read reports, wrote articles, while other theatres in the country quietly appropriated the ideas of Craig, publishing them as their own' (Stanislavsky, 1945:523).

Craig's ideas for set design were based on a philosophical concept rather than a particular interpretation of a play. He later admitted that the screens had been unsuitable for *Hamlet*, his son Edward, wrote, 'He realized that he should never have attempted to use his screens for the play at all – it was like trying to play a piece of music on an instrument for which it was not composed' (Arnott, 1975:77). In this production the mechanics of the set failed the design, though Craig's influence on Russian set design was apparent soon after. In 1924 in Moscow, 1925 in Tbilisi and 1926 in Baku, one after another, three premières of *Hamlet* took place. The first two were undoubtedly linked to the by-now-renowned Craig–Stanislavsky *Hamlet* of 1911. The Tbilisi production placed the screens on a revolving disc (an improvement on Craig's innovation), behind which was the bleak shape of Elsinore and an enormous stairway, leading to the castle. It was on the stairway that the principal scenes took place, symbolising 'all the life and movement of a man, his ups and downs' (Rudnitsky, 1988:279). In Baku, the director Alexander Tuganov transferred the tragedy's action to a kind of abstract oriental country. To all the characters, except Hamlet and Ophelia, he gave Muslim names, and he designed the set in a Persian-cum-Turkish style. The Azerbaijani dramatist Dzhafar Dzhabarly (1873–1941), who had translated and edited *Hamlet* in accordance with Tuganov's oriental tragedy, was convinced that he was guided by Goethe's view of the necessity of applying the works of Shakespeare to the conditions of a given stage, meaning that the place of performance has a precise effect on what is performed there. In a letter to the director Dzhabarly expressed satisfaction that the play was acted out against a background of the East and everything down to the most minor detail was oriental. The critics agreed that there was little sense in presenting a Danish Elsinore, as this would reduce its 'universal significance to nought' (Rudnitsky, 1988: 178–9). These three productions all started from the same text and the same scenic inspiration, but nevertheless they remained very different from one another.

The theatre set as an environment is a modern concept and it has much to do with the rise of particular types of theatre building. During the late 1960s and early 1970s in Britain an attempt was made to take the theatre building closer to our idea of an Elizabethan stage: Chichester Festival Theatre in 1962; Sheffield Crucible Theatre in 1971; the Olivier Stage, as part of the Royal National Theatre in 1976; the Victoria Theatre, Stoke-on-Trent, in 1962; and the Manchester Royal Exchange Theatre in 1976. The theatres at Chichester, Sheffield and London used an open thrust stage form, the Stoke-on-Trent and Manchester theatres were theatres-in-the-round. Several stages around the country with proscenium arches were adapted and modified, for example the Royal Shakespeare Theatre at Stratford-upon-Avon. The stage itself became the symbol of a separate world and the absence of set paradoxically became a presence, a statement about the relationship between theatre and the world, the stage and the auditorium.

At the Royal Shakespeare Company (RSC) Buzz Goodbody conceived an idea to produce Shakespeare in a single environment. In 1975 she directed a much-acclaimed production of *Hamlet* at The Other Place, the RSC's third theatre space in Stratford, which was opened in 1974. Goodbody, who led the company in the productions there, mounted productions on a shoe-string, with the total budgets ranging from as little as £50 to £150. For the 1975 *Hamlet*, Chris Dyer's set was minimal and the audience was included in the environment: a raised shallow platform against white screens, ramps at the side and a kabuki-style bridge running through the audience to the rear. The setting was environmental in the sense that it happened all around and the audience were seated in an area which the actors used as an additional playing space. The screens served as an arras, and clicked back and forth like a camera shutter for the entrances and exits, overlapping like baton changers in a relay race. The sliding screens could form a continuous neutral-coloured wall or when open (which was rare), they could provide a central entrance or recess. An occasional table or stool furnished the set at relevant moments – Polonius at his desk, Gertrude at her dressing table. The costumes were modern dress. Hamlet always kept the audience in view, sitting on the edge of the stage, talking to them as confidants, and the action took place all around. When Laertes returned to the castle he slammed the actual theatre doors, implying further that the whole space was Elsinore. The simple staging demanded simple effects and when the Ghost first appeared it was at the back of the auditorium, spotlighted from the stage by the torches of the Danish police (Marcellus and Bernardo). The disappearance of the Ghost was executed equally as effectively. Hamlet stood behind the audience and, like watching a tennis match, the audience's attention moved from the Ghost to the prince; by the time their gaze returned to the Ghost, he was gone. The activity of the audience meant that they effectively participated in making the change. For the dumb show, the Players wore plain white masks, and again the scene was spotlit by a player in the central gangway: when Polonius is killed he falls to his death dragging down the whole arras/curtain, simplifying the removal of the body, ready-wrapped as it were, at the end of the scene.

The role of the set designer has gradually become more prominent over the last one hundred years, particularly through the work of Craig, so that by the 1960s, the director's closest aide in any theatrical presentation had become the designer, whose involvement and influence on a production is now paramount. John Bury, designer at the Royal Shakespeare Company in the 1960s, defined the function of the set in a Shakespeare production as basically involving 'a fluid framework that will not impede Shakespeare's swift changes in location and time, and . . . the correct symbol that will place in the mind of the audience the vital image of the play concerned' (Bury, 1966:56). How do we differ-entiate between an environmental setting that symbolises a vital image and one which does not? Ultimately, categories matter little, as a further distinction of the images and concepts can be made in relation to the play in question. The 1992 Barbican production of *Hamlet*, played by Kenneth Branagh, was designed by Bob Crowley. Set around 1900, it had a look of Scandinavia reminiscent of the plays of Henrik Ibsen (1828–1906). The Ghost made his first appearance emerging through the soil of a small untended cemetery, which was located downstage and remained in view throughout the play. In this design we move from the formal columns of the court to Polonius' office, stacked floor to ceiling with filing cabinets. Ophelia's bedroom is presented with painted nursery furniture. The Players' acting area is downstage with dressing tables (in the wings) visible to the audience. The Players perform with their backs to the audience, as they face Claudius and the court, who are seated in a replica theatre that fills the false proscenium with full-scale seating. When Ophelia's nursery becomes a landscape of dead leaves and flowers before her suicide, the action opens out to the full stage depth. This, in turn, becomes the duelling ground for Hamlet and Laertes and the final moment when the Ghost receives Hamlet's corpse. The production was reviewed as offering 'dozens of unforgettable images' (Herbert, 1993:41).

The 1991 production of *Hamlet* by the British touring company Cheek By Jowl, and designed by Nick Ormerod, brings us full circle, to a utilitarian approach. In an open stage space Ormerod designed a small platform stage. This replicated the kind of stage a touring troupe may well have put together for a performance in a great hall or nobleman's house. By the use of cloths and curtains it became different places. It had a curtain attached by the actors for the Players' scene. It became the battlements, the court, and Gertrude's bed when covered with a red bedspread. Above, a canopy was moved on pulleys to create different spaces for different scenes. There was a stage cloth hanging upstage as a backing to the whole of the stage. For the queen's closet, another cloth was added for the arras. All the changes in the setting were carried out by the actors. The staging was simple and the platform stage gave the production a specific sense of its own space, no matter what style of theatre building it played in. It also located the performance symbolically, as the actors on entering the stage space climbed onto the platform to suggest they were performers about to embark on the telling of the tale of *Hamlet*. The design moved swiftly and the canopies had the effect of sweeping the next scene on stage. This style of presentation is most suitable for touring.

The third Globe Theatre was built on the south bank of the Thames in 1992–7. The dimensions of the original Globe, having been discovered nearby, have provided enough information to build a replica of Shakespeare's theatre. Yet, even with the recent archaeological find, the question remains of how a play by Shakespeare should be staged. The panel of designers and academics argued over this very point, for instance, in determining the width of the doors at the back of the stage. In finding an answer, the committee took into consideration modern staging requirements, as the building is to be used as a performance space and not as a museum. The designers wanted the entrances to be high enough to allow actors to enter, carrying banners and spears, and to enable them to be backlit and shrouded in smoke, to evoke the movement of army troops. The academics argued that this consideration would make the dimensions incompatible with the Globe of Shakespeare's time. This debate illustrates how any building structure may change due to dominant aesthetic aspirations. When money and time was available, the Elizabethan court performances were extremely elaborate. In contrast, Cheek By Jowl's preoccupation for its production was with the van size and the cost of the available resources.

As you have read, directors and designers have come up with a number of methods of staging *Hamlet*. The main problems lie in the pace and number of scenes in this long play, which can run to three hours, and even up to four hours for those productions most faithful to the text. Perhaps the first job to be carried out by a director will be to cut *Hamlet* to the size most appropriate to the cast, playing space and any other constrictions, including the budget. After cutting the play, the primary concern will be the need for the number of different locations. These practical considerations continue to determine production aesthetics.

EXERCISES

Character Indicators

You might find it interesting to look at specific clothes and accessories and work backwards towards the character. This method clearly illustrates the process of designing the costumes for characters and, I think, shows the drawback in making simplistic choices.

What sort of person would you associate with:

- a grandad shirt with separate wing collar
- a gold fountain pen
- a tartan shopping bag
- a suede jacket
- a pair of stiletto-heeled shoes

The income bracket of the individual, their friends and hobbies, will lead you to build a character. This exercise may even be the way you begin devising a project for performance. Your world immediately becomes peopled.

Measuring and Fabrics

The cutting and making process is highly skilled but I hope you will be able to begin to make costumes which are appropriate to your work by following some of the techniques laid out below.

The first part of the making involves measuring. It is standard practice to take all the following measurements of each of your performers, which can then be stored on record cards. There are ten basic measurements points for the upper body (see illustration).

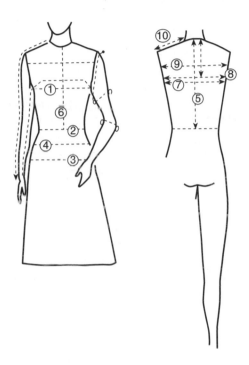

Figure 3.3 Where to take measurements

1 Bust – around the fullest part of bust, ensuring tape measure does not slip down at the back.
2 Waist – around natural waist line.
3 Hips – around the fullest part of hips, approximately 20 cm below the waistline.
4 Upper hips – around hip bones, approximately 10 cm below waistline.
5 Back length – from nape (back of the neck) to waistline.
6 Front length – from base of throat to natural waistline.
7 Back width – from armhole to armhole, about halfway down back.
8 Chest – around body, above bust and under arms.
9 High chest – from armhole to armhole on the front, approximately 10 cm below the base of the throat.
10 Shoulder – from neck point to point at which arm begins and shoulder finishes.

Take measurements closely but not tightly. All vertical measurements should be taken on one side only and all horizontal measurements should be taken with the tape measure parallel to the floor except in the case of the chest measurements, when it finds its own level. Lastly, measure the figure over the undergarments to be worn beneath the finished garment.

The amount of material required will vary depending on what has to be made: The following guidelines are based on a 38-inch (965 mm) chest, male or female:

Modern shirts with long sleeves – 1 yard (914 mm) × 72 inches (1829 mm)
Knee breeches – 1 yard (914 mm) × 72 inches (1829 mm)
Pantaloons – 1½ yards (1371 mm × 72 inches (1829 mm)
Tail coat (French Revolution) – 1¾ yards (1600 mm) × 72 inches (1829 mm)
Frock coat (Victorian) – 2 yards (1829mm) × 72 inches (1829 mm)
Plain short tunic (Saxon) – 2 yards (1829) × 72 inches (1829 mm)
Sleeveless skirted doublet (Tudor) – 1½ yards (1371 mm) × 72 inches (1829 mm)
Female houpelande, full length with hanging sleeves (medieval) – 5 yards (4572 mm) × 72 inches (1829 mm) plus 1½ yards (1371 mm) for sleeve lining
Wheel farthingale gown (Elizabethan) – 4¾ yards (4343 mm) × 72 inches (1829 mm)
Crinoline gown over hoops (mid-nineteenth century) – 8¾ yards (8001 mm) × 72 inches (1829 mm)

Many of these examples belong to a historical period and will require you to embark on further research as to the look you wish to design. It is rare to slavishly follow a style even when you are attempting to re-create a sense of period, as you will be working with different fabrics. As with styles of dress, fabrics have their own period and nationality. Here are some examples:

Chintz – from Hindi 'chint'; originally any printed cotton fabric, now a drapery fabric with a glossy finish.

Challis – named after the Native American term 'shalee', meaning 'soft', this is extremely soft plain or twill weave fabric with a faintly ribbed texture. Woven from fine wool or cotton thread.

Georgette – a semitransparent material with a crepe weave. Woven from silk or fine Egyptian cotton yarns, but now usually synthetic.

Jute – natural fibre taken from the jute plant and used since prehistoric times.

Pongee – a lightweight, natural-coloured, textile, usually of silk, with an irregular texture in a plain weave.

Twill – a weaving technique resulting in a strong diagonal design. Also a general name for

---

Health & Safety

The curtains flown in for the Capulet's ball in Sheppard's *Romeo and Juliet* were made of dyed pongee, which were inherently fireproof. Often fire officers have to test fabrics on stage by doing a burn test. The burn test for silk is that the fabric is self-extinguishing – it burns briefly then chars and the flame shrinks.

When you order materials for scenic use, as opposed to costume use, manufacturers can tell you if the fabric is flameproof. If it is not, you can buy a liquid such as Flamebar to make it flameproof.

any fabric with a distinct diagonal cord in its texture. Some examples of fabrics with twill weave are wools, cashmere, cotton, denim, ticking.

Worsted – a general term for yarns that are tightly twisted and extremely smooth. It is also used to describe fabrics made from these yarns and is used to differentiate between smooth-textured suits from shaggier woollens.

Mask-making

You can use a clay model or a wire mask. The clay model can be made using Plasticine or clay to model the shape you require. Allow the clay to dry and then put Vaseline over the surface. For a quicker mask, you can build up tissue paper over the model. Then on top of either the tissue paper or the Vaseline start building up the layers of papier-mâché. A layer of butter muslin, a plain weave cotton fabric, on the fifth layer will strengthen the mask. Six layers in all should be enough. When this is dry, prise the mask off the model. Be careful not to damage the model if you want to use it again. Paste the edges over into the back of the mask. Cut out eye holes and paste the edges smooth. You can then sand the mask with fine sandpaper and paint over with shellac. This will bind any loose pieces together. Pierce holes for elastic. Paint and add embellishments as appropriate. In the same way, you can use hard hats, models for head pieces, motorcycle helmets, or even lamp-shades, to make a base for a larger mask.

The wire mask is the stronger of the two. Using wire, create your frame and then attach papier-mâché as appropriate. The clay model can be used to create a plaster of Paris mould. Made by mixing the plaster with water, it dries like a china mould and lasts longer than a clay model. This will give you a negative image of the mask.

Here is a list of materials which you may find useful for mask making:

Buckram – useful for making helmets and headgear.

Muslin scrim – fine mesh for sculptural details and as a reinforcement for plaster moulds.

Plasticine – for general purpose material and models.

Clay – ideal for mask models.

Papier-mâché – or fine paper pulp.

Plaster of Paris – for moulds from the clay positive image – also known as alabastine

Sandpaper or glasspaper – for sanding; comes graded between coarse and very fine.

Epoxies – compound adhesives for strong fixing, usually slow drying.

Contact or impact adhesives – brought together when a little dry; very difficult to move afterwards.

Latex glues – excellent for fabrics, paper and card; quick drying brands like **Copydex** very successful.

Polyvinyl acetate (**PVA**) – a form of wood glue which can be bought in bulk and can act as a glue or when watered down can glaze a surface for protection. It is a popular medium for mixing powder colours.

Polymenthyl acrylate (**Acrylic**) – used as a painting medium and adhesive for fabrics and paper.

Shellac – a varnish for stiffening felt and for waterproofing and hardening masks and props.

Also useful is a collection of tapes – parcel tape, masking tape and clear tape – with string, cotton and synthetic threads to provide embellishments and **reliefs**, a sculptural effect which gives contour and definition by the projection of features from a flat surface, so that they are wholly or partly free of it.

Costume Solutions

Your costume choices need to be informed by an initial idea – the concept and approach to the production you are undertaking. Some researchers of theatre studies have begun to write about the open nature of costume, as I have implied in the exercise 'Character Indicators'. If you are making an original piece of theatre you may begin by creating a costume from which you develop ideas and a character for the performance. If this is possible, then it proves that the information we display through costume is understood by our audience and therefore these indicators must be thought about clearly and precisely. Below are some ideas which you may want to use to develop a costume, either on a small scale or to develop that idea into a full costume concept for a performance.

- Use of material as costume
- Use of garment as costume
- Use of accessories as costume
- The cardboard box, bin bag and orange box
- A lab coat with meringues
- Plastic fruit
- Computer parts
- Breaking down costume

The only limitation to how you make your character or mask, and how you go about it, is your imagination.

Site-Specific

In 1996 Nona Shepphard was approached to write, direct and produce a community project for the Year of Opera and Musical Theatre in the east of England. The adaptation of stories from the *Mahabharata*, an epic Indian poem about the struggle between two rival families, was originally an idea by Kadam, a Bedfordshire dance company which had suggested the project to the Eastern Arts Board. The project was to be a collaboration between artists and the community, providing the latter with a sustainable base from which future projects might emerge. The concept posed an enormous challenge, however, and the productions were only possible through the effort of a great many people, who gave their enthusiasm and expertise to the dream that this epic work could be translated to the stage and made accessible to a broad audience in Bedfordshire, Hertfordshire and Lincolnshire.

During 1996 the project faltered due to a lack of finance and the ever-decreasing time allowed for the involvement of the local communities. In an ideal world the project would have held regular workshops in the

Site-specific

'Site-specific' is a relatively new term which describes any space where theatre may occur other than a building built specifically for performances. In recent years there has been a trend for theatre companies to work in a variety of buildings, such as churches, schools and factories. In some cases these venues have later been made into permanent theatre spaces. However, site-specific performances usually refer to performances which have been made for and are played in one space only for a short period of time, and the performance space itself is integral to the production. The terror and the joy of site-specific performances lie in the many fortuitous events and unforseen disasters which can occur and which you simply have no control over.

course of a year, when skills in areas of performance would be taught: dance, voice and acting; and areas of technical theatre, lighting, set, costumes and sound. However, rather than workshops, *Bed of Arrows* provided a large production process for those communities which became involved and were undaunted by the time-scale of the project.

The Text

The use of the *Mahabharata* as the text had many advantages, notably a source book eighteen times as long as the Bible. However, given the breadth of the work, which contains many separate episodes, the difficulty lay in deciding what to leave out while ensuring the success of a coherent theatrical event. Shepphard's previous work has involved both commissioned plays and adaptations and her work is primarily known for its accessibility and its epic nature. In the end she chose to concentrate on the stories of four women and follow their progression through the tale towards the Battle of Kurukshetra. This decision was somewhat revolutionary, offering, as it did, a female perspective, because the tales more often focus on the experience of men. Shepphard's other concern was the need to be faithful to the culture of India. This was achieved through research into various Indian writings; a visit to Madhya Pradesh and Rajasthan; and generally immersing herself in Indian source material from art to literature, all of which undoubtedly helped Shepphard to present a true flavour of India.

The Venues

The plays in the trilogy are *Shaft of Sunlight, Eye of the Moon*; *A Quiver of Husbands*; and *Bed of Arrows*. *Shaft of Sunlight, Eye of the Moon* was performed for three nights in 1997 at the Palace Theatre, Watford, a proscenium arch theatre with a small apron stage which is slightly raked. It had a three-week rehearsal period and was comprised of summer-school participants at the theatre who were aged between thirteen and twenty-five.

A Quiver of Husbands was a collaboration between the Year of Opera and Musical Theatre and Kadam, which works in Bedfordshire schools and in the community, primarily teaching dance. Sujata Banerjee and Sanjeevini Duta, directors of Kadam, provided the community network in Bedfordshire and Banerjee choreographed this episode using textures from Kathkali, a form of dance drama, and Bharatanatyam, traditional Indian folk dance. It was performed in 1997 at Bedford Corn Exchange.

Kathkali

Kathkali is a dance form which uses gesture and expression. It has specific movements and steps which communicate character and emotion in a conceptual and literal sense. In this respect, it is a codified form of physical communication.

The last play, *Bed of Arrows*, is comprised of two distinct parts: the first part involved four performances of the women's stories in their tents in the battlegrounds at Kurukshetra; the second part was the battle itself. The production was staged in the grounds of Lincoln Castle, with the Law Courts as the backdrop to the battle. This performance was bedevilled with bad weather but succeeded in playing for two nights in early July 1997, with a platform performance at the castle in late July. A broad section of enthusiastic participants included the local Indian dance troupe Idama, the Lincoln Kofukan Karate Club and a yoga group.

On the day when all three parts of the trilogy were performed at Queensway Hall in Dunstable, the companies from the three counties were brought together, playing to an audience of seven hundred. At the time of the performance this 1920s hall was due for closure and was in pretty poor condition.

Technical Challenges

The initial challenge stemmed from the budget, which was set at an overall amount of £92,000. However, when production costs were calculated, it was found that the project could not be completed for less than £126,400, which broke down as follows:

FEES/EXPENSES	£54,350
DUNSTABLE	
Meal allowances:	£2,500
Transport of participants:	£2,500
Total	£5,000
TRANSPORT	
Watford (provided by the theatre)	
Bedford:	£500
Lincoln:	£1,000
Dunstable:	£500
Total	£2,000
CREW	
Watford (provided by the theatre)	
Bedford:	£500
Lincoln:	£1,000
Dunstable:	£1,000
Total	£2,500
STAGING	
Lincoln:	£1,000
Dunstable:	£1,000
Total	£2,000
HIRES	
Sound:	£5,000
Lighting Watford:	£400
Lighting Lincoln:	£2,000
Lighting Bedford:	£750
Lighting Dunstable:	£1,000
Total	£9,150

SET, COSTUMES, PROPS	£15,000

EXTRAS AND OTHER STAFFING

Costume supervisor:	£1,500
Extra administration:	£2,000
Community liaison:	£3,000
Community ASMs expenses:	£1,600
Two extra ASMs for Lincoln:	£700
Total	£8,800
MUSICIANS	£9,200
ACTORS	£18,400
TOTAL	£126,400

This sum was needed to produce three-large scale productions and the show in which all three productions would be played together.

The venues for each performance had very particular features. The first was the Corn Exchange at Bedford, which is a large hall with a flat floor and retractable seating, and a fixed balcony, and is used for a variety of events, from concerts and recitals to council meetings. The performance space was 5 metres deep and 16 metres wide; there was no backstage area. A complicating factor was that the production week was in May 1997 and a general election was held on the day before the show opened. This meant a get-in on a Monday, the completion of the technical rehearsal on Tuesday, and dress rehearsal on Wednesday, followed by a get-out on Wednesday night, as the hall was to be the main vote counting centre in Bedfordshire. That count was completed on the Thursday and a refit was scheduled at noon for a final dress rehearsal, before our first performance the following afternoon. The production included fifty members of the local community, who had other commitments during the day, and the evening rehearsals were therefore very pressured.

The professional staff working on the show were a designer, a lighting designer, stage manager, assistant stage manager, a production manager, six actors, a director and a producer. At the venues the personnel running the rehearsals were the director, stage manager, and lighting designer. The designer only got to see the second show, as she spent much of the time making the costumes for the fifty performers.

The set was very simple and contained three sets of hired access ladders, which had wheels and a brake system. They formed the major features for choreographed set changes, helping to transform the nature of the stage space. The ladders were used throughout the trilogy at the different venues and helped to lend some continuity to the design and style of production. At Bedford we also rigged some inexpensive **paper rope**, which is paper twisted to look like rope. The designer had dyed the rope in different colours, which helped transform the Corn Exchange into our performance space. The performance had large set pieces of dance and had to allow for large-scale movement of the performers and the ladders, leaving no space for any further staging.

The director, designer and lighting designer talked about the look of all the productions in terms of colour, texture and atmosphere. Much of the discussion ranged over the subject of India and its culture. It was important that the set evoked this sense of place in a simple and easily achievable way.

In Lincoln, the castle grounds were to be the place of performance, and performances outdoors have a host of other challenges to contend with, not least of which is the weather. During production and its preparation, liaison with the castle authorities and groundsmen was essential, as well as the local council, from which permission had to be sought for the use of the public site, and the police, who had to cordon off the gate area.

The story to be told at Lincoln had a very different style to that in Bedford. The Lincoln show also had the most performers, with a full orchestra, a junk band, a karate team, a Kathkali dance school, and a specially gathered group of local amateur performers, in total, around 120 people, all of whom needed to be stage-managed.

Lincoln Castle grounds are walled and contain a courthouse and a museum. The grounds are landscaped, with many trees, shrubs and pathways. In this part of the trilogy the four women are isolated from one another in individual tents, which were to be very specific to the women and to their families. Here the audience learns of the conflict between the Pandavs and the Kauravs. The budget did not allow for the tents to be made and so marquee tents were borrowed from various Boy Scout troops in the area. Three were intact, but the fourth came only with its canvas, and some branches had to be lashed together to enable the tent to be erected.

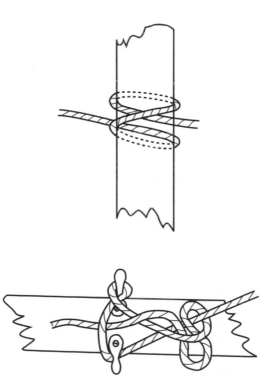

Figure 4.1 Clove hitch knot (top) and cleat knot (bottom)

Control Rooms

The Control Rooms for Bedford, Lincoln, Watford and Dunstable were all entirely different. In Bedford the lighting and sound operation took place from the balcony surrounded by the audience. At Lincoln the operations were perched at the top of the towers that formed the entrance into the battleground. The tents all had localised operation. Watford had a traditional control room with a glass window through which to see the stage and at Dunstable there was a small window just large enough for the end of the follow-spot to poke through. However, there are some general rules for the control room which you should try to maintain no matter what kind of control area you have. There should be no casual conversation during a show. The communication system should be used solely for running the show. No eating, drinking or smoking is allowed in any control room in case of accidents to the equipment: liquid spilt on a lighting board or sound desk can cause thousands of pounds worth of damage. Once the run of the show is completed, the control room along with other areas such as dressing rooms and the stage, should be cleared of all goods, props and rubbish belonging to that production. For safety, comfort and hygiene, all control rooms should be kept clean and dust free.

On the day of the fit-up it rained continually for nine hours, and by lunch time it was decided we should go ahead despite the conditions, in order to avoid a serious delay in the schedule. By 10.30 in the evening all four tents were erected, with the set, sound and lighting equipment safely stored inside. It rained all night, and in the morning the makeshift tent was found collapsed under the weight of the water. All in all, over the production week some part of the set had to be re-erected each day.

Two of the tents had sound and video projection and all of them had lighting. The castle is often used for rock concerts, so mains electricity was available to each tent and there was a main rig to light the Act 2 playing area in front of the courthouse. There was also a full sound system to balance the microphones for the orchestra, junk band and singers. For key points the performers had radio microphones. Around the Act 2 playing area there were coloured smoke pyrotechnics and large flashes for the beginning of the Battle of Kurukshetra.

The last play to be rehearsed and performed was in fact the first part of the trilogy. *Shaft of Sunlight, Eye of the Moon* was produced in Watford at the Palace Theatre by the Youth Theatre under Shepphard's direction. There were twenty-five participants. Here we had the support of a theatre infrastructure but still a minimum budget within which to complete the work. Like the other two productions, the design features were maintained in terms of colour and style of costume. Welded sculptures hung above the stage space, representing an eye and a moon. The character Amba had been for many years a recluse in a forest, and her environment at night was simulated with the use of cheese graters and candle holders wired for electricity and lit with small bulbs. These props became major features of the design (see fig. 4.6).

Dyes were used to create a coherent design for all three episodes. By dyeing all the cloth herself, the designer was able to buy large batches of material, which saved money. She also made some interesting and innovative use of car mats for armour. The chairs which were needed as thrones were canvas director's chairs with material thrown over them and peacock feathers for decoration. The chariots were built from hospital linen

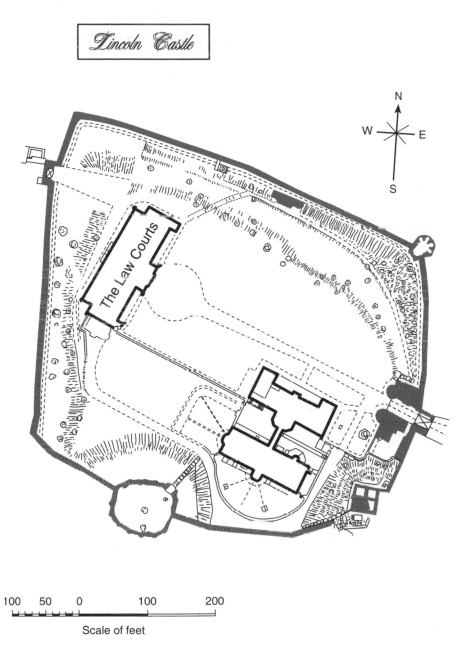

Figure 4.2 Lincoln Castle: the grounds show the courts, the walls and the museum building.

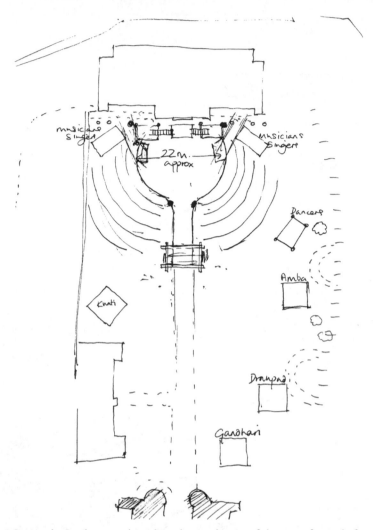

Figure 4.3 Lincoln Castle grounds and production layout of the tents for *Bed of Arrows*.

cages with large wooden cable drum wheels. The life-size elephant, which appeared carrying a small child at the Battle of Kurukshetra, was made from withies and papier-mâché. It took seven people over three weeks to build and was a spectacular sight. It travelled to Dunstable on an open forty-foot flatbed trailer, and now lives in the community centre at Lincoln.

Dyes and Dyeing

There are a variety of dyes, from shop-bought cold water dyes to dry pigments which can be mixed. The latter allows a greater range of colours and shades, which can be applied to different parts of cloth. There are aniline dyes and tinting dyes and these must be used

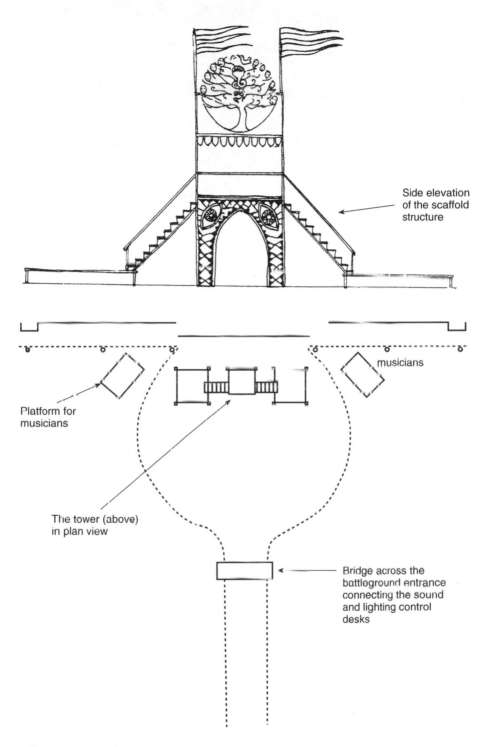

Side elevation
of the scaffold
structure

musicians

Platform for
musicians

The tower (above)
in plan view

Bridge across the
battleground entrance
connecting the sound
and lighting control
desks

Figure 4.4 Battle area in front of the Law Courts in *Bed of Arrows*.

Figure 4.5 Sketch of the side elevation of the tower in front of the Law Courts in *Bed of Arrows.*

with vinyl or acrylic binders. It is important to understand how to make and use different binders. **Size** is one of the most traditional forms of binder. It is an animal glue, used as a bonding medium for **pigment**. Paint consists of three parts: pigment, which is the colouring agent; **binder**, which adheres the pigment to the surface of the material; and **vehicle**, which is the binder's solvent and evaporates when dry. So paint is pigment held in suspension in the vehicle.

   Dry pigment is the basic colouring agent of all paints and is relatively cheap. Mixing can be difficult and most unstable colours should be used carefully, for example the earth colours, natural and almost all the dye colours, and pigments which contain mineral or chemical pigment. As a general rule, however, a little liquid detergent or methylated spirits will alleviate mixing problems. The clarity and intensity of colour in good quality dry pigment far outweighs these minor problems. In mixing the dry pigment, always put fluid to powder never the reverse. Mix the colours into a thick paste with cold water and thin out to a working consistency, like a thin cream, with liquid size or prepared emulsion glaze: 0.5 kg of colour when mixed with size or emulsion glaze will cover about 5 square metres. Emulsion glaze is prepared by mixing one part glaze with three parts water.

   Acrylic pigment is a supersaturated paint produced by Rosco and is easier to work with than dry pigment, as the binder is already mixed in. The range of colours, however, is limited and it is more expensive than dry pigments. Many scenic artists prefer Rosco colours for speed, while prop-makers prefer dry pigment.

   Bronze powders are powdered metallic pigments, which can be mixed with any binder, but glue binders tend to dull them, as do coats of glaze. **Shellac**, a ground beetle varnish, works well but is more expensive.

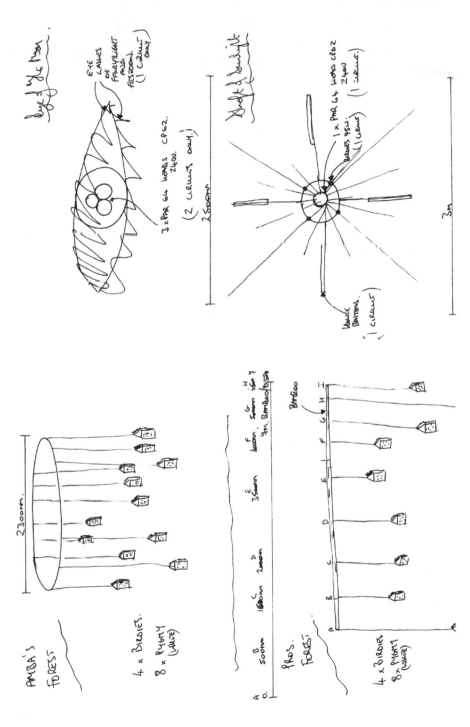

Figure 4.6 Working sketch of practicals for eye, moon and forest made from weldec pieces of metal with cheese graters, candle holders and other light fittings.

The application of size has a number of uses. As well as mixing pigments, it can be used to **prime** surfaces. The purpose of sizing, or **priming**, is to fill the pores of the fabric or wood, to tighten the fabric and hold it taut, and to give a suitable working texture to the entire set. It becomes size only when a binder, such as glue or vinyl, and a vehicle, such as water, are used. A **prime coat** consists of a mixture of size and pigment, which creates the basic colour tone, very close in colour to the **base coat**. If scenery is primed, it should only need one base coat; if only sized, it will need two. As this procedure sets the quality of the surface on which all other painting will be done, it is an important one. After priming, we can then **cartoon** in the design using charcoal. The cartoon is the outline of any pattern or picture. A design may include a repeated pattern, or a raised pattern. **Pounce patterns** are often used on a repeating design or in some cases where the patterns are very complicated. Holes are punched into paper using a **pounce wheel** and a **pounce bag**, which is a piece of cheesecloth filled with powered charcoal. The charcoal is rubbed or tapped against the paper to transfer the design. **Inking** refers to a weak solution of Rosco. Traditionally aniline dye was used, but aniline is quite volatile and dangerous to use. So with the advent of supersaturated pigments, it is now unnecessary to use aniline dye to outline designs. Inking or using pounce patterns is particularly suitable when painting gauzes.

Painting Techniques

A floor cloth needs a thin coat of any type of size and then a light priming coat. Canvas takes all kinds of paint well but it receives dye poorly unless it is well primed. Using an overhead projector you can project a design onto the floor cloth. Projection is a speedy and efficient way of transferring a design but has the drawback of creating a slight distortion at the outermost edges of the image. The more traditional method of transferring a design is by **squaring up** using a **chalk line** or **snap line** (make sure you use string coated in charcoal because carpenter's lines with red or blue chalk can prove impossible to remove). Charcoal can be easily **flogged off** canvas. Mark the design in squared sections and transfer these squares to scale to your cloth. For example, each square on your design could be worth 30 cm when scaled up. You could make the scale 1 metre but the smaller the squares, the more accurate the finished cloth will be. Use the snap line to create the grid over the cloth. You can then cartoon the design using both the grid on the cloth and the grid on your image as guides.

Walnut effect: as with all of the examples given here, it is best if you are working from a picture or photograph, as a sample of the desired result. Interior design magazines are extremely good references. Walnut-effect can be achieved by using a base coat of white and then mixing two batches of glaze, one with Raw Umber and the other with Raw Sienna. Paint these in patches on the base coat. Wipe the brush clean and gently brush over the entire surface to blend the two colours. Now fold a soft cloth to make undulating ribbon shapes, or crumple the cloth to make a less regular but similar effect. Make sure you leave spaces between the ribbons and then stipple the in-between areas with a bristle brush; varying the size of brush, twist the brush to make knots in the 'wood'. Then soften the entire area rigorously in different directions. Once you are pleased with the effect, varnish with a gloss of eggshell glaze.

Mahogany effect: paint a glaze of Burnt Sienna and Magenta Pink over a dirty pink base coat. Use a stronger mix to paint over central and corner areas. Wipe the brush clean and brush the surface to blend the colours. To mark in the grain, make an arch shape with a dry stiff brush or **grainer**, which is also called a **comb**. Keep the comb at the same angle throughout and leave no gaps between the arch. Soften the resulting flame effect with a dry brush.

There are many different marbles and this technique is for a **Breccia Marble effect**. You will need Raw Umber and a white base with a glazed finish as your base coat. Mix the following colours very thinly: Raw Sienna, Brunswick Deep, French Ultramarine and Magenta Lake. Apply very thinly to the surface, spreading the glaze as far as it will go. Wipe away angular pebble shapes with a soft rag, leaving thin areas between. Vary the sizes of these shapes to get a strong dynamic design throughout the work with squashed thin shapes as well as large freer shapes. Softening the work is difficult because of the thinness of the glaze and patience is required. When the work is dry, begin to draw veins through the marble with a long-haired sable brush, encircling them with angular veins and sometimes veining across other veins. Soften the work again and emphasise some areas more than others. Leave some areas quite plain.

For an **Oak effect** a white base coat with Raw Umber is needed. Paint on the glaze using Ultramarine Blue, Raw Umber and Titanium White. Drag up and down. At intervals mark the glaze with a triangular and graduated comb. Use a **heart grainer** at infrequent intervals. Pull down the triangular comb diagonally to make ticking marks in the vertical grain. Use this over the heart grainer to break up the heart grain you have created. When the glaze is nearly dry, flog it upwards. Try to produce lights with your thumb or a cork wrapped in cloth or with the triangular comb wrapped in cloth. Flog again to even out the texture.

All these techniques require practice. You may want to try to use some of them in the Flat Project, set out in Chapter 11. They have been used for centuries to great effect. Many come from the theatre craft of scenic artistry practised by the Greeks and the Romans. Scenic techniques must be used with an attention to detail and consideration of the appropriateness to the atmosphere and scene you wish to create. For site-specific work you should consider the distance of the audience from the setting, as this will help to maintain the illusion of painted sets and three-dimensional features.

CHAPTER 5

Changing Spaces – the Use of Dynamic Scenery

This chapter deals with two plays, whose performance spaces are transformed during the course of the performances. Both shows involved a process of moving from tangible worlds with floors, walls and objects, to unknown worlds, shadowy and insubstantial. In *A Happy Medium* the transformation occurred as part of the action and the audience experienced the change; in *Café Vesuvio* the transformation happened in the interval and the audience returned to find that the whole auditorium had changed. It is interesting to consider the different impacts the audiences experienced by being present for or absent from the transformation.

Case Study

A Happy Medium by Nona Shepphard
- George Bernard Shaw Theatre, London (1993)
- Director: Nona Shepphard
- Designer: Marsha Roddy
- Lighting: Christine White

A Happy Medium is a play which was developed through the process of **devising**. It began with the subject of death and the afterlife, which was explored by Shepphard and a group of student actors from the Royal Academy of Dramatic Art (RADA). In a closely collaborative process, the designer and lighting designer made contributions in rehearsal, offering their thoughts and ideas. The designer set up a mask-making session through which the actors could explore their other identities for the afterlife.

The Text

The story concerns a spirit medium, Janet Briggs, who has travelled to a town in order to give a talk about her work. She is well known and has written many books on the afterlife and on her own life as a medium. We see her arrive in her hotel room, which has not been made ready for her. She meets various members of the hotel staff, from the hotel manager, who apologises for the inconvenience, to the cleaner, who only

---

Devising

Devising is a term which describes a method of creating work through improvising around a subject, idea or style of performance. It can be difficult to decide what kind of technical support may be necessary for such performances, unless certain desired effects are established during the devising process. Do not be tempted to think that such effects can be fitted into your technical rehearsal. The technical rehearsal is a time for the practice of techniques and the successful integration of those techniques into the performance. It is not a time to be first thinking about solving a staging problem. Necessity may be the mother of invention, but if you give yourselves longer to think about design and technologies during the rehearsal process and do not procrastinate over the decision, your invention will be refined and more effective. You will need longer to practise new techniques until they become second nature, like riding a bicycle. The relationship between all the people involved in creating successful theatre needs to be one of collaboration and common aim. The skills and application of a variety of theatre arts are necessary and must be competently completed. Theatre arts rely on aesthetic conceptions conditioned by practical execution.

---

speaks Sinhalese. The medium is due to give her talk that evening; she never arrives, and is confronted instead by a sequence of events played out by the hotel staff, events which reveal that she is dead. She had been hit by a car crossing the road to the hotel. The people she has met are spirits themselves, helping her to make the transition to the other world.

Technical Challenges

For *A Happy Medium* the set had to simulate a hotel room which could mysteriously disappear in such a way as to seem incredible. Transformation scenes have been part of theatre practice for centuries and often involve a great deal of theatre machinery to make them work. For example, in the court masques of James I, Inigo Jones designed many transformations that resulted in the flying-in of gods and fairies, and huge pieces of scenery. In the nineteenth century Henry Irving used transformations within his productions which were highly spectacular, in part to attract an audience but also to fully utilise the theatre's transformation facilities, such as trap doors, flying systems and gauze cloths. Lucia Elizabeth Vestris (1797–1856) used such devices in the work of J.R. Planche (1796–1880). She made innovations in costume and scenic design in what became known as burlesque extravaganzas. There is some dispute as to whether she was the first manager to use a box set, thought to be either in 1832 at the Olympic Theatre in London, or in 1841 for *London Assurance* by Dublin-born dramatist and actor, Dion Boucicault (1820–90).

The designer for *A Happy Medium* produced a set that gave the appearance of a box set but which could be collapsed later in the play as part of the action. This allowed us to be transported beyond the substantial world to an ethereal place, created with sound, masks and light. What was necessary came directly out of the text, which developed throughout rehearsal.

The play was performed in the George Bernard Shaw Theatre, London, which has very little space on either side of the playing area. The set had long white **cotton casement**

Figure 5.1 *A Happy Medium:* this scene shows the large attic window and the casement curtain.

curtains, which hung on each side to hide the wing space, with a huge attic window to the rear and a doorway on stage right. The window had lengths of the same cotton casement hung in front of it. In order for the set to collapse, a door flat was made to fold into the window area and the window to fold in half. The door and window were wooden structures, built like flats. The bottom of the window had wheels behind it, making this section a truck, which had stage weights in the bottom so that the whole structure, when folded, remained balanced. The curtains could then be drawn to reveal the bare bricks of the theatre and the whole set piece could be trucked off into the stage-right wing space. The curtain was then re-drawn. This transformation left a large empty space where once the hotel had been, which solved the staging from a practical point of view and was emblematically in keeping with the themes of the performance.

Case Study

Café Vesuvio by Nona Shepphard
- Royal Exchange Theatre, Manchester (1999)
- Director: Nona Shepphard
- Designer: Marsha Roddy
- Lighting: Christine White

The Text

This is the story of Parminder, a girl from Manchester whose family is from the Punjab in north-west India. She visits Café Vesuvio because she has heard about it from her grandfather, and she makes friends with Lillo, the boy who lives there. Lillo's Italian grandfather and Parminder's grandfather had been business partners who had quarrelled.

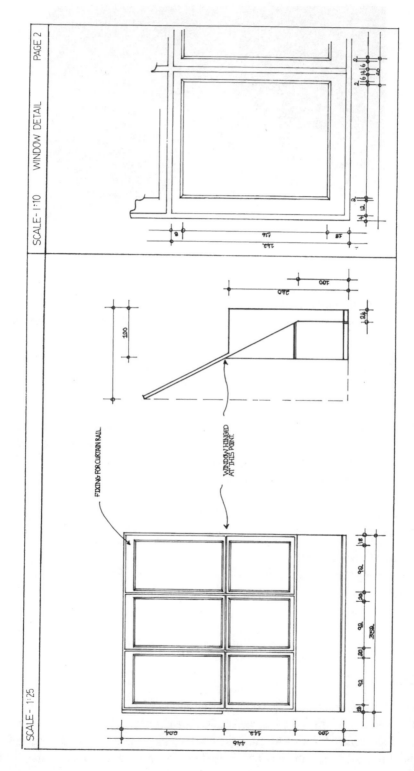

Figure 5.2 Set plan for the folded attic window in *A Happy Medium*.

Figure 5.3 *Café Vesuvio* set showing the fridge cabinet and rear glass shelving trucks.

Parminder's grandfather left a riddle for her before he died and she arrives at the café with his ashes. The riddle leads both young people into the centre of a volcano, whose entrance is in the café. By the time they reach the centre, they have uncovered secrets about themselves and their parentage.

Technical Challenges

Café Vesuvio was commissioned by the Manchester Royal Exchange Theatre, and was performed in the studio, which, like the main theatre, is in the round. Like *A Happy Medium*, this play also requires a change of space. This time it was neatly separated: in Act 1 we are in the café; in Act 2, the volcano. However, we had to be back in the cafe for the denouement. During their time in the volcano Parminder and Lillo meet the Virgin Mary and the god Shiva. The inside of the volcano had to be hot and noisy.

For the café, the director and designer chose those features which would most simply and evocatively indicate such a place. There were few set structures, and so what was chosen had to be very particular and detailed. There was a fridge cabinet and an espresso machine, and two tables, each with two chairs. In the first design there was also a door flat but it was felt that it was unnecessarily cumbersome, given that it would have to disappear and then reappear at the end. The clearing away of the café was not a problem, as this could occur in the interval between the acts, but getting it back mid-act for the end of the play was more difficult. Naturally a theatre in the round does not offer the chance of a curtain, but even in a different stage space the use of a curtain to hide the change would have been inappropriate for the action because it would have changed the pace and dynamic of Act 2, when the audience is being lead to the dramatic consequence of all that had gone before. Nineteenth-century theatres frequently used a device for just such a transformation known as an **act drop curtain.** Music was usually played while the change was being completed. This style of transformation is rarely seen in contemporary

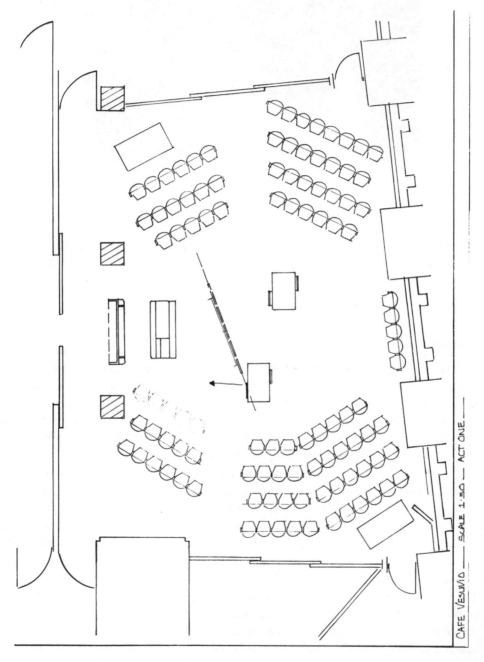

CAFE VESUVIO — SCALE 1:50 — ACT ONE

Figure 5.4 Ground plan for *Café Vesuvio* set; Act 1 – in the café. Note the audience arrangements.

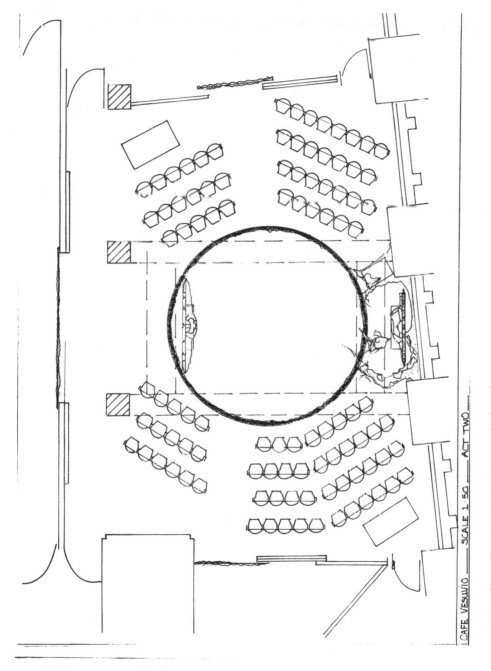

Figure 5.5 Ground plan for *Café Vesuvio* set; Act 2 – inside the volcano.

theatre productions, as, quite rightly, it is felt to impede the pace of the show at crucial moments.

The change to the volcano involved **trucking out**, which, in this case, involved wheeling off the fridge counter and clearing the tables and chairs. The audience was asked to leave and then gauzes were hung over the doorways to the theatre space (see illustration of ground plan, fig. 5.5).

The theatre had a fly tower in the centre of the playing space and so lights – practical café lights – could be flown in and were rocked when the volcano erupted. Bunting was flown in for the flashback to the opening of the café. Both movements were achieved with normal flying bars with hemp rope attached to them, which moved over pulleys and was tied off on a cleat. The Virgin Mary and Shiva descend from bridges to meet Parminder and Lillo. They had to be strapped into a harness and then lowered on steel lines attached to electric motors. These are often called **turfers** and are used on building sites to move heavy loads. The motors are attached to the bars and the steel lines run over pulleys. All this equipment needs to be locked onto a structure which is safe and secured. Usually this is a rigid support joist (RSJ), which in some theatres forms part of the **grid**, which is the arrangement of metal beams from which the pulleys are mounted for the flying system. In theory, the studio theatre at Manchester does not qualify as a flying space in the traditional sense, like, for example, the Leicester Haymarket, which we looked at in Chapter 2, but by using these flexible motors in an existing roof space effects can be achieved. Extra time was scheduled into the technical rehearsal in order for the actors to practise getting into the harness and onto the platform, and for checking the speed of the motors with the actors on board.

The staging of *A Happy Medium* and *Café Vesuvio* amply illustrate the way in which scenes and all that is contained within them visually contribute to the play in performance. There is no right or wrong way to produce either of these shows. Productions in a variety of different styles and spaces can be imagined; but the choices which are made will change how the audience engage with the performance.

Language of significance and the creative process

It is quite hard to find a language to deal with the description of dramatic effects, especially if you are trying to identify how such effects affect the spectator. When we watch films, an interpretation can occur which breaks down the film into sections. This is partly enabled because we see films as a series of discrete pictures, images or frames. We are treated as individuals receiving the film. The art of the film-maker is to create frame after frame of well-placed objects and actors, often juxtaposing them in order to enhance meaning within the frames themselves. Film directors focus our attention on any individual signs and icons they wish us to 'read'. The film-maker can also provide further signs, using particular styles of editing, and as spectators become more familiar with the film, they begin to recognise these signs as a convention. In other words, the code of information can be gradually short-circuited, as the spectators become used to viewing the style. For example, if when watching a horror film we hear strongly orchestrated music, a sense of suspense is increased which often builds to a moment just before the hand/object/monster grabs the victim. All of this can be well-defined in terms of signs, which have a distinct effect on the spectator, and the spectator can, in turn, decode that information.

The theatre is neither created nor received in quite the same way. We do have certain rules that can be followed which are guaranteed to create certain atmospheres. They can be called clichés of the style, like the music in the horror film. However, the effects often work on a level of recognition which is greater than cliché. If a cliché is used cleverly and disguised within the theatrical production by a new context, then the audience will experience the desired effect without feeling that they have been easily manipulated. Live performance of any nature is a communal and ritualised event. It is expected that we will be influenced by our neighbour spectator. Performers often comment on the difference between audiences during the run of a production, and despair if the audience is small, as the show will be a different one from that played in front of a full house. In reality, however, a warm small house can be much better than a cold full one. At any rate, what is notable is the great amount of communication going on between the live performer and the spectator. This is often changed by the surroundings in the theatre and whether those surroundings are conducive to creating an atmosphere where people are encouraged to remain as individuals or experience the production collectively as an audience. The environment which is created will have a significant impact on the audience. Consider how differently we behave when we are in a doctor's waiting room or a public bar.

We often hear people speak of an intimate theatre environment, and theatre in the round engenders those feelings of intimacy. Most theatre auditoriums should be designed to make the audience respond in a collective way. Ideas of the collective consciousness professed by C.G. Jung (1875–1961) are pertinent here. Jung's theory relates to a global collective consciousness and he suggested that the unconscious is never at rest. He used the example of dreams, which very often contain images and thought associations which we do not create with any conscious intent. On the contrary, these ideas arise spontaneously, and, as such, they represent psychic activity. The psychic process, like any life process, has a purpose and dreams can give us an interpretation of life expressed in this kind of spiritual phenomenon. As part of the creative process, Jung writes of the ability of a person unconsciously to put together images or ideas which have a parallel meaning. He calls this Crytomnesia, 'the unconscious recollection of a thought which the dreamer had once read somewhere.' However, he also suggests that this cannot always explain such coincidences. One belief is that human beings do tend to work in terms of archetypal behaviour, which can only be recognised if we have inherited those ideas. According to Jung, archetypes are mental pictures, common to all people, and frequently appear in art and literature. If these archetypes only occur in dreams, then, the theory goes, they must be inherited thought patterns. Therefore the unconscious must contain not only personal but also impersonal collective components in the form of inherited categories or archetypes. This is the stuff that theatrical cliché is built upon.

Jung found it interesting that the unconscious processes of the most remotely separated peoples and races show a remarkable similarity, which is displayed in the similarity between the themes and forms of autochthonous myths, that is, myths which are indigenous to humanity. The universal similarity of the brain yields the universal possibility of a similar mental functioning. Hence the collective psyche. In those few remaining primitive tribes the chief or healer of the tribe is seen as an individual with certain totems to add to their mask, such as props which are features of their role in this society. Physical masks can be used as a means of enhancing the personality. The mask then performs a social function; it helps to remove the individual from the collective and this removal can be magical. When physical masks are used in theatre, their physicality and the lack of similarity to the human face allows the moment a poetic or universal quality or magic.

From this it may be presumed that our personal response is bound up with the collective response. However, the point at which any image or idea is understood is difficult to pinpoint. The kind of symbolism that is found in dreams has features which belong to the collective consciousness. This knowledge allows us to understand the nature of the shared experience in the theatre and the way in which we are engaged by the live performance. In addition, this is informed by our repetition of behaviour and playing out through imitation specific stories that confront the individual during his or her lifetime. Theatre continually uses imitation as a method of production, but what is being imitated? When the audience recognises the imitation, do they learn from it and imitate it again? Is the process of performance what we do normally or can it be an investigation of things we have never experienced?

According to Jolande Jacobi in his *Psychology of C.G. Jung*, 'The dream represents an actual drama in condensed and simplified form and readily lends itself to a breakdown according to the order underlying classical drama'. From this, we might draw the conclusion that archetypal images can generate creative energy. They engage the audience and through the successive additions of the audience's own ideas to the initial symbol or image – the audience makes the final outcome infinitely more complex. Each member of the audience simultaneously responds to the live performance with his or her personal understanding of what is occurring on stage, as well as responding to what is presented as part of the collective unconscious.

Many truths are transmitted through expressionist, impressionist and symbolic forms. The English poet and painter, William Blake (1757–1827) suggested that symbols have the power to evoke the world beyond our senses and by this reveal the inner elements of rhythm and pattern which are the means by which we distinguish one living thing from another. Whilst the wearing of masks in classical theatre transcended the living present by discarding the limitations of time and place, the actor's stage identity was real. The mask is so far removed from our own reality that it potentially allows us to see universal truths. Artists engaged in creative theatre reformulate life which is staged for consumption by the audience. The symbolic power of the performance is its ability to extend itself and multiply its references, resulting in a complex pattern which we may at once call real and describe as symbolic.

Ibsen asserted that his plays were full of symbols because the real life he strove to imitate was itself full of symbolism. Maeterlinck states in his essay 'Le Tragique quotidien' that 'the poet's task was to reveal the mysterious and invisible qualities of life, its grandeur and its misery, which have nothing to do with realism. If we stay on a realistic level, we remain ignorant of the eternal world, and therefore of the true meaning of existence and destiny, of life and death.' These writers used different styles to contact their audiences but they understood that what they portrayed in live performance would be symbolic and would potentially also have mysterious qualities. As theatre artists, we must try to use images and create atmospheres which are appropriate to our own individual understanding of the texts we are working with, and appropriate also to the collective understanding of the team which is creating the live performance. The French playwright Jean Cocteau (1889–1963), who indulged in the playfulness of visual puns, believed that the 'The true symbol is never planned, it emerges by itself'. In the creation of designs for live performance and technical solutions to creating a place to play, you must allow ideas to emerge and be alert to influences from the world in which you live.

Theatre buildings and spaces of performance have various qualities and difficulties for the practicalities of production. The history of theatre practice is often related as a history of theatre buildings and we are continually trying to find the perfect architectural space for theatre performance. However, no matter how many permutations there are in relation to technology and space, the basic premiss always involves a choice of space for the performance and a choice of space for the audience. The arrangement of these spaces or, indeed, the intermingling of these areas, alters the practical and technical needs of a performance. There is no rule, anywhere, which says you must use lighting, sound or set for live performance, but the actors most likely will need clothing, and in live performance this will become costume. If you are working indoors, or outdoors at night, your performance will require some form of illumination. In the twenty-first century lighting, and sound reproduction and reinforcement through the use of microphones, have become features of live performance. After the Second World War many new theatres were built and equipped with the latest technology In the 1960s and 1970s the touring theatre groups travelled around the country to different venues, often using small vehicles or even public transport. This had an effect on the style of scenography which was possible. The venues generally all contained some lighting units and means of operation and some method of recording, playing and reinforcing sound effects, and so production costs could be kept to a minimum. Both sound and light have the ability to delineate and harmonise the stage and audience spaces. They are plastic arts which can be used as interpretative tools by practitioners, and as the technology for both developed, their use became more adventurous. Sound and light can be used realistically, metaphorically and symbolically to alter mood in the audience and their sense of place. Lighting can also be used deictically to direct the audience's attention to the area, object or performer which are to be highlighted. Lighting performs a directorial function in this respect, for without the light the audience cannot see what it is to concentrate its attention on.

Approaches to text

The scenic directions outlined by a playwright form a blueprint for theatrical production. The methods by which we foreground specific references, perhaps by using lighting, sound and set, complement other elements of the performance, such as language and production. The scenographic features are not just the mechanics of the illusion but allude to an atmosphere and style which are significant. Therefore, spoken language and physical sets together create a new language which continues and extends the language of live performance.

In the 1960s and 1970s performance events, sometimes called 'happenings', had a great deal of influence in breaking down the traditional architectural distinction between audience space and stage space. Tadeusz Kantor (1915–89), the Polish designer, director and visual artist, created happenings in an autonomous theatre, in which actors are used as props and mannequins and the text exists on a par with the other components of the production. In the 1970s he developed his Theatre of Death, where he appeared as a master of ceremonies. His play *Dead Class* (1975) brought him international acclaim. Avant-garde artist Allen Kaprow (1927–) staged his *18 Happenings in 6 Parts* in the Reuben Gallery, Greenwich Village, New York, using multimedia technologies and low technologies. Here members of the audience were given instructions of what to do at the ring of a bell, becoming themselves additional performers interacting with the performance. Given the gallery location and the ensuing audience participation, a new stage–audience relationship was created.

The relationship between text and space is integral to the theatre practitioners' choice, and in contemporary theatre this often leads to a struggle to find a different yet suitable architectural relationship that is appropriate to the dramaturgy being developed. To devise a new theatre building, which by means of mechanisms would offer a diverse range of scenography and encompass works ranging from classical Greek drama to that of contemporary authors, visual artists and performers is not a possibility. In fact, many performance spaces cannot facilitate your ideas; the challenge to the scenographer is to make an imaginative leap to represent those ideas. The influence of the visual has become paramount, and thus, as this realisation has seeped into mainstream production, so the importance of scenography has at last been recognised. The need to engage with and free the imagination is key to any practitioner's work in the theatre, for an imaginative response is yet another way of seeing and thinking about the place of human beings within the world. Grappling with these thoughts and dilemmas in terms of scenographic production is a relatively new challenge and one which Swiss stage designer Adolphe Appia (1862–1928) outlined in his theatre practice and writing:

> In philosophy, psychology, and the like, we give such phenomena technical terms. This does not alter the fact that all could be reduced to the term 'to imagine', for all of them imply an image before their realization. These facts are well known, yet we do not utilize them in those phases of our existence where imagination could be of great service. This indifference distorts and lowers our scale of values; for, in order to evaluate, the object of evaluation must be understood or invoked by imagination. ... One wonders whether it is not urgent to admit imagination as a specific branch of academic instruction or, at least, to encourage it by pointing it out and conferring upon it a very high value.   (Appia, 1922: 364–5)

Live performance is also changed by traditions which have grown up through different theories. Richard Wagner was single-mindedly dedicated to the art of music-drama. The total work of art for which Wagner used the term *Gesamtkunstwerk* referred to the theatre production in which all arts were to find expression. He felt that the nature of live performance should have unified audio and visual features, with the performers as the central interpreters. This led to his requirements of a darkened auditorium and, in his opera performances, the orchestra being placed beneath the level of the stage and so out of the audience's sight. The result was that the image portrayed on stage became more and more like a picture frame or a window, through which the audience looked at the event played out in front of them. This type of theatrical layout has enabled spectacular effects to be achieved, the mechanisms of which can be concealed behind the proscenium arch. The fully equipped theatre building with mechanical and electronic devices allows many permutations and changes in the scenography presented on the stage. However, many of the new technologies are based upon and developed from older devices, mechanisms and techniques of staging, which have originated in many different cultures for over two thousand years.

In general terms there has been a move away from the traditional box set and the scenography of the twenty-first century is a very mixed and plural world of theatre. The practitioners are more concerned to discover a meaning which they wish to convey, and through an abstract presentation, lead us to a universal truth. In many ways this approach emphasises the theatricality of theatre, offering as it does the quality and atmosphere of the world which the performers inhabit. In this respect the essence of the stage space lies in its incompleteness: the audience is required to fill in the gaps. These sets are then charged with expectancy and await the performer who will become a part of the scenographic whole.

CHAPTER 6

Small-Scale Tours

From the 1960s small-scale tours have been a means of getting new work to audiences in a number of geographical locations. These tours often consist of a small team of actors, with one, possibly two, stage managers. Technically these tours can be especially interesting, not least because of the inventiveness of the design in its relationship to the text, while taking into account the logistics of transportation. In other words, the question you must ask yourself is whether all your ideas will fit in the van, with the actors as well. Such limitations have a bearing on both budget and design. It is necessary to embark on a comparison of the venues to be visited to establish if there are common features which may prove problematic for the production. It may be that only one venue in the tour will pose some difficulties, which can range from lack of equipment to the show being dwarfed by the size of the building. It is essential to consider means by which the show can be supported in these different spaces.

The spaces you are likely to tour to and their geographical locations are often not under the control of administrators of touring companies, because although it makes sense to play in roughly the same area as you progress around the country, companies must take bookings where they can. However, it is clear that a performance in Penzance cannot realistically be followed the next day by one in Edinburgh, so some common sense must prevail. Travel is less exhausting and money can be saved on van hire, petrol and even accommodation if a number of venues can be covered from a central base. An additional challenge is the need to ensure that the show can arrive intact at a venue in the early afternoon, get-in, fit-up, and be ready to perform at 7.30 p.m. The day ends with the get-out and loading of the van. The company then sleeps and drives to the next venue the following day. This is a tough schedule for all concerned and the actors and stage manager will work as a team to put together the show's set, costumes, lighting and sound.

Forward planning is one of the key features in any tour. A list of **technical specifications** from all the venues is essential, giving details of lighting and sound equipment (including a comprehensive technical explanation of that equipment) and a **ground plan** of the performance and auditorium space. The latter is a scale plan showing the exact position of all items on the stage floor and indicating the position of any items suspended from above.

In order to communicate technical requirements, many touring companies complete and send a **technical specification form** (see sample over) to the venue. If you are performing in a non-theatre space or a site-specific venue, you must find out what restrictions, such as fire regulations and audience management, need to be taken into consideration. Every space will have regulations, some may come under the local authority codes but most importantly you must find out before you start any design or rehearsals

Technical Specifications

DATE PRODUCTION

Delete as applicable and give as full a description of your requirements as possible.

- State equipment requirements and list your personnel and their duties:
- State auditorium configuration, number of seats, if forestage is required, rostra. Also give details of your set, with ground plan.
- Give information about your lighting and sound designs and a deadline date when these will be ready for the technical staff to see. (This should be a minimum of seven working days before your get-in and should be presented in plan form.)
- Do you require special effects in your production? If so, what and how long is the duration of their use?

SIGNED BY..
ON BEHALF OF THE COMPANY

what the limitation may be, as these codes may change what it is possible for you to do. If you do not find out in advance, a fire inspection or risk assessment on the night could close your show before you have started.

A touring company must state clearly the number of workers it requires from the venue's staff; its lighting and sound requirements; the stage management team which it provides for the production and their duties; the auditorium layout; the number of seats to be sold; any use of rostra which they do not provide; any special effects used in the course of the production, for example the use of candles, smoking or any other naked flame; the use of pyrotechnics, stroboscopes or anything peculiar/particular to the production. Again, these are subject to the approval of the technical staff at the theatre and may have to be ratified by the local fire and/or health and safety officer. The use of pyrotechnics in the form of loud explosions, gunshots and strobes have to be prefixed by a written warning to the audience. This should be placed in a prominent position where it can be read before the audience enters the auditorium. If you are uncertain about any of the requirements for your show, talk to the technical staff at the theatre well in advance of your production week. The engagement of a fire officer to approve your performance has to be booked in advance. Pre-planning of this nature will avoid disappointment.

Some venues may have to supply equipment to a number of other venues and so cannot guarantee that the equipment listed will always be available. And some will not have equipment at all and you will need to hire whatever is essential for the production. All this information enables you to get a sense of the places you will play in and what you can reasonably expect to find when you get there. In designing for a small scale tour, you must start with the sense that you need to create a particular atmosphere which is related to your show. What matters is your ability to transport your audience, with the help of their imagination, to the places and atmospheres which you feel will support the performance, regardless of the venue housing the production.

The productions in this chapter have one thing in common: they played in small venues around the United Kingdom. *The Lady Dragon's Lament* and *100 Million Footsteps* also played in schools. *Crazy Lady* had a much shorter run – a one-night stand at The Lawns in Lincoln, three nights at Leicester Haymarket Studio, and a week's run at the Drill Hall in London.

Case Study

The Lady Dragon's Lament by Nona Shepphard (1994)
- Director: Nona Shepphard
- Designer: Marsha Roddy
- Lighting: Christine White

The Lady Dragon's Lament, a one-woman show performed by Nona Shepphard, was played in schools and theatres – from a small school in Croydon to the main auditorium in Manchester's Royal Exchange. It toured with two people, the performer and one stage manager, in a specially adapted Mercedes van, capable of touring the set and eight actors. On a couple of occasions the show did two shows during the schoolday at different venues. The ability to get-in and fit-up quickly, ready for performance, and to have a set which would not look strange in these widely differing venues was key.

The Text

The Lady Dragon wants to set the record straight about dragons, lamenting how they always come off worst in their struggles with humans, of whom she has a poor opinion. She tells the story of her meeting with Little Pal, her friend, whom she betrays for diamonds, rubies and emeralds.

Little Pal is a **puppet**: the designer made three clay models of the head from which she chose the final one and then cast that head in plaster. The plaster mould was then filled with a **latex** mix, which rendered the face pliable and soft and, gave it a skin like feel, enabling the actor to give the puppet different facial expressions. Latex is used in the manufacture of rubber and it comes in liquid form; it can be thinned with water. Once the latex has set it can be painted and glazed. The puppet's body was made from velvet material and his hair was made out of strands of chenille wool. His arms were padded and wrapped in the same velvet material and as he talked to the Lady Dragon he could have his arm around her neck or sit with his hands clasped in front of him. This added to the life-like quality of the puppet and the believability of his character.

Technical Challenges

The set for *The Lady Dragon* was very simple – three orange flats backed a large painted floor cloth, on which were placed two boxes. The lines of the set were very clean and had a Japanese simplicity, matched with beautiful colour tones. Its classic design made it fill a small venue and stand out in a large one. It was also important that the actor could achieve every change on her own. The 8 feet × 4 feet flats were covered with

> **Puppets**
>
> Puppets have been used in theatre for centuries and this generic term refers to hand puppets, like Little Pal, shadow puppets, which are two dimensional profiled shapes usually performing in silhouette against a white screen, and marionettes, which usually have strings and/or rods by which the operator can move the puppets' limbs. Some of the most expert puppet-making takes place in the Czech Republic, which is renowned for its puppet theatre.

stretched canvas and painted using Rosco supersaturated paint and a spray gun, which allowed the colour to be built up gently in order to get a graded effect. A versatile material, canvas comes in off-white and other colours; it is an open mesh fabric usually of linen but more frequently the term 'canvas' refers to a heavy cotton scenic fabric. Most flats are now covered with **plywood** and occasionally canvas is glued to this to provide a texture for painting. Plywood comes in various thicknesses but always as 8 feet × 4 feet sheets, and the number required will be based on the sheet size. Most often plywood will be painted or textured, so the quality of the finish is not important for theatre applications.

To canvas a flat take the wooden frame and lay it either on the floor or across some workbenches at waist height. Then lay your canvas over the top of the frame and, using a staple gun, staple at the mid-point of each of the four sides of the canvas nearest to the outer edge of the frame. Pulling the canvas taut, work from top to bottom and then from side to side. Next, glue the canvas onto the frame, making sure the canvas is attached and taut all the way around. You will need to clamp this in position until it dries or add more staples to the outer edge of the frame, which can then be taken out once the glue is dry. When dry, pull the canvas over the sides of the flat and take it round the back. Trim the canvas to cover the remaining flat edge. Again, staple or clamp until the glue is set and then pull out all the staples. After priming, the flat is ready to paint.

A linoleum floor cloth was used for *The Lady Dragon*, which had been painted many times by the company for different shows. Three lengths of this cloth covered an area of 6 m x 6 m and was fixed to the floor with **dance tape**, a clear strong tape. A design of the Buddhist symbol was painted on the floor. The boxes were made using a bracing structure and faced with ¾-inch plywood. One was decorated with a Celtic design and was made to withstand the weight of the actor, and two long piano hinges allowed the sides to be opened fully to reveal the dragon's treasure inside. The other box was similar in size and designed to look like a wooden freight crate, which contained other items and props necessary for the plot. Both boxes were constructed to reveal surprises to the audience as the story unfolded. Although they were a known feature of the design before rehearsal, the way in which they were to operate was not. This developed out of rehearsal and the designer had to be sensitive to solving the technical problems of staging the plot development with the actor.

Case Study

100 Million Footsteps by Di Samuels (1997)
- Director: Guy Holland
- Designer: Phil Engelheart
- Lighting: Christine White

The Text

100 Million Footsteps had a cast of four actors who played a variety of musical instruments, and one stage manager. The play was set in the fourteenth century and followed the story of a young boy who sets off to join the Children's Crusade because he had no other purpose in life – he had no family; he was cold and hungry. He meets up with other children from different backgrounds and comes across a range of cultures and religions – Christianity, Judaism and Islam. We see young people praying to their God and being convinced of the superiority of their faith over others. The children's crusades began in France, although it is thought that some children left Britain to join them. They roamed over Europe, crossing the Mediterranean and travelling into the Middle East.

Technical Challenges

These vast geographic areas clearly could not be presented in a realistic way, so the designer and the lighting designer worked with the director on features which were evocative of time and atmosphere.

A floor was designed as a **raked platform**, built on metal struts, and textured and painted to look like rusted iron. A wooden platform was bolted securely to the frame and the rake was inclined towards the audience. Around the edge stood miniature sheep, which, at the beginning of the play, the boy shepherded. Behind the platform was a screen, which worked like a **cyclorama**, and it was shaped to contrast with the floor. Normally a cloth which extends around and above the stage, the cyclorama in this show was a smaller set piece rather than a standard item (for a more detailed description of a cyclorama and its uses, see p. 83). Beyond that was a black velvet starcloth containing **fibre optic** threads, used to simulate stars. The threads are usually forced through the cloth and held in position with specially designed clips. The loom of fibres is then attached to a box which contains a light and sometimes a wheel which interrupts the flow of light to the fibres, thus giving the effect of stars twinkling.

The raked floor helped to define our playing area. However, although the angle of the stage gave the performers a presence, it was difficult to walk on. Raked stages occur in many large-scale theatres, for example the Theatre Royal, Drury Lane, London.

The painting technique for the surface of the platform involved **profiling**, the cutting out of wooden shapes, which, when laid on the surface of the rake, created dips and ridges to suggest pockets of decay. Initially the designer suggested there should be water in these pockets, like puddles. This proved too expensive to achieve, however, as the floor would have needed to be waterproofed and the damage to costumes would have involved a large amount of wardrobe maintenance, for which there were not facilities at some of the touring venues. Instead we used a technique

Theatre Royal, Drury Lane

Theatre Royal, Drury Lane, London, was originally constructed in 1663, and over the next 150 years it was rebuilt three times, in 1674, 1794 and 1812. Some of the buildings were literally built on top of their predecessors, as they declined in business or were burned down. All were dedicated to providing scenic excitement and the stage area was huge.

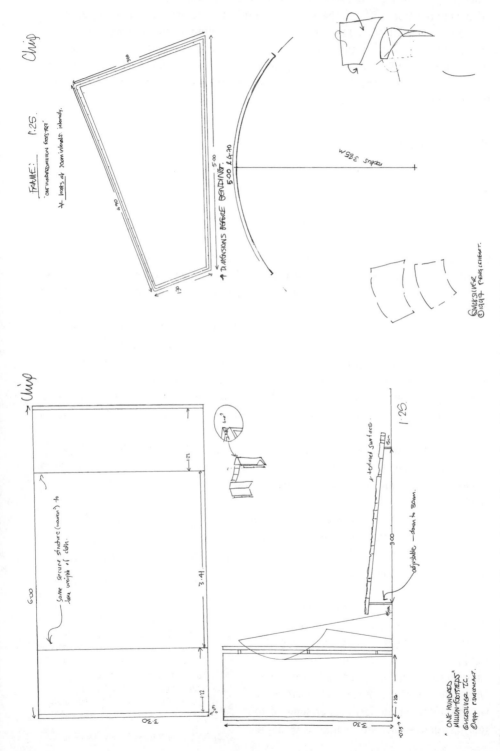

Figure 6.1 A sketch of the raked flooring in the side elevation with the cyclorama in *100 Million Footsteps*.

which gave the appearance of rusted metal. This was achieved by overlaying many different colours, mostly strong reds and oranges. The final coat was glazed with polyvinyl acetate (PVA). The key for any depth of effect is to build colours over one another.

The show also used **projection**, with a very small projector hidden behind the white screen cyclorama. Any number of materials can be used to create a projection surface, however there are a number of materials which are better for this purpose than others. The screen designed for the show had a specially made frame which could be erected and dismantled rather like a frame tent. It had metal pipes which were cut in sections. A spring inside each section kept the correct pieces together. The sections could then be snapped together to form a longer section of pipe on which the projection screen could be hung. The canvas material is stretched over this frame. The stretched surface is usually white, as this helps to reflect the light and produces a clear projected image. Some screens can be manufactured to provide extra luminance, the amount of reflected light from a surface.

A number of instruments can be used to project images, the most obvious being a theatre lantern. Profile units can hold **gobos**, round metal pieces which can project the designs which are cut out of them. Basic **slide projectors**, like a **carousel**, can be used which may hold a number of slides. Dissolve units for these projectors fade at different rates between one slide and another. Or, for simple effects, an *overhead projector* (OHP) can be used to operate a moving effect similar to a **diorama**, as the acetate is rolled from one roller to another. A diorama is a backcloth which is on a set of rollers standing vertically at the back of the stage. By turning the rollers the backcloth moves across and so the horizon and landscape painted on it moves also. As the cloth moves from one side of the stage to the other the audience gets the illusion that any action happening on stage in front of the landscape is moving and the speed of movement of the cloth needs to be aligned to the movement of the performers in front of it if the illusion is to be believed. This technique was very popular in the nineteenth century. More sophisticated projection effects can be created using the more expensive Pani Projectors and Barco Projectors (see p. 127–8).

In *100 Million Footsteps* we used 2 Solar Projectors, which are small projectors often used for display cabinets and exhibition effects. They have glass or plastic wheels of different designs and you can also design your own images and slot these in the wheels. For this show we used a cloudy blue sky effect, along with a number of projected gobos and moving gobos. Moving gobos can be achieved by placing a moving wheel on the front of a theatre lantern. This is called an **animation wheel**, and literally animates the image that is on the gobo.

> **Gobos**
>
> Gobos are pieces of metal which can be put into profile lanterns to create a projected pattern with light. They can be made from thin aluminium or purchased readymade. Clear artwork is essential for the best quality images; standard patterns are available and the range is very wide. You can often get an effect with a gobo which has been designed for another purpose. For example, you can use cloud gobos for break up and texturing the light without focusing them so sharply that an audience will recognise the pattern.

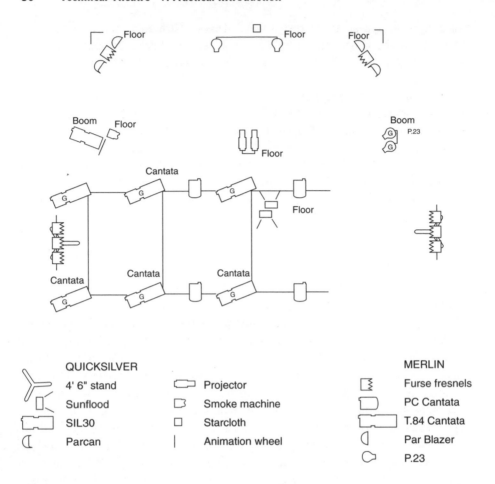

Figure 6.2 The lighting plan for *100 Million Footsteps* showing projectors and lanterns with gobos.

The wheel is an aluminium disc with patterns cut out of it. If, for example, the gobo has an image of leaves, the animation wheel can make it appear as if the leaves are falling. If the image is of slashes of light, this can look as if rain is falling. This is the cheapest and most effective form of moving projection.

In this production the actors and the costume changes were in full view of the audience. Without being simplistic or reductive, the costumes were designed to be indicative of the cultures and countries the children passed through. This is a key problem with any kind of presentation of costume, which can indicate culture, period and nationality, especially if you are trying to maintain an artistic aesthetic and coherent visual experience. The musical instruments provided the music for the show and also became part of the set. Some of the instruments not only sounded beautiful but looked wonderful, especially the dulcimer, a tuned percussion instrument consisting of a set of strings stretched over a sounding board and struck with a pair of hammers.

Case Study

Crazy Lady by Nona Shepphard (2000)
- Director: Nona Shepphard
- Designer: Christine White
- Lighting: Christine White

The last show I want to discuss in this chapter is *Crazy Lady*, an interesting project because the idea for the design came from other sets and props that already existed, as the commissioning company had very little money for a budget. This is a method of production that you will most likely use for your own work. However, if you are fortunate in finding suitable looking objects to be used on stage, always examine them closely to ensure they accord with the style of your production.

The set consisted of three lengths of silk, which had been dyed for Shepphard's production of *Romeo and Juliet* (see Chapter 3). These formed a backcloth to the stage space. Five **torch stands** were also used from *Romeo and Juliet*, fitted out with new mechanisms and mock flames. The furniture and props were all found. You can often pick up the items you need from second-hand shops and charity shops. The offer of free tickets or free advertising may tempt the more reluctant shop worker to lend some items to the company.

The lighting for *Crazy Lady* made great use of the existing practicals. The design thus resembled a theme bar very similar to London's Bar Humbug in Brixton, which has a gothic feel with low level lighting and very dark corridors. It has a mix of furniture from different styles and periods but all made of wood. The tables have candles and the spaces in the bar are separated by heavy, patterned curtains. So even in a production where all the items were found there was a reference for the way the bar should look.

Imitation torches and mock flame effects have become popular features in wine bars, hotels and restaurants. This show performed in Lincoln and most of the rig was placed on the floor, as there are no high lighting positions,

Torch stands

These were made by using metal conduit as the main structure. Conduit is metal pipe which is used for electric cables and can be bent into different shapes. This formed the main stem of the torches with a wooden base large enough to house a battery and a top structure which simulated a cresset for the flame. A cresset is a receptacle for oil in which a wick is dipped to burn. The rest of the stand was textured with paper rope to suggest other metal structures which held the cresset. The stand was painted to look like rusting wrought iron. The paper ropes and conduit were covered with masking tape and papier-mâché to produce a surface that would take the paint. The flame was created using a 9 V fan and a 12 V dichroic bulb: a strip of magnetic tape was attached to the fan and another strip was attached to a triangular piece of silk measuring 38 cm high; the light was covered with some orange and blue coloured **filter** or **gel**. The effect suggested a large flame, as the silk, catching the light, was blown by the fan.

which added to the gothic look. However, at the Leicester Haymarket and at the Drill Hall, the rig needed to be larger to accommodate the different viewing points of the audience. Both these venues had raked seating and so the sole use of floor light would have meant that the faces of the actors would have been extremely dark and difficult to see, as the audience would have looked down on actors who were being lit from below. Whilst this look was desirable, it was balanced with lighting from above.

The set altered according to the different facilities of the venues. In Lincoln and Leicester the silks were a seamless backcloth which the actors slipped through. However, because the grid height and the width of the stage in the London venue was large, it was possible to separate the silks and provide spaces for the actors to enter and exit easily. This gave a greater sense of the capacity of the huge, empty bar. There are three characters in the play – two old friends and the bar owner, a woman and who sits in the corner and plays the cello. The desired atmosphere was to be one of strangeness, so we hung the cello, a cymbal and drumsticks from the grid on **monofilament**, or fishing line, in such a way as to make these items seem to be suspended in midair.

Unlike the Leicester audience in the small studio space, the London audience viewed this strange world from a distance, which more closely suited the essence of the play and greatly enhanced the audience's response to it – a clear demonstration of the way in which the relationship of actor to audience can change the nature of your show and its reception.

The production budget was £900, including van hire, petrol and running props. Here is a breakdown of the expenditure.

PRODUCTION BUDGET: CRAZY LADY

STATIONARY £	LX (LIGHTS) £	PROPS £	VAN HIRE £	PARKING/PETROL £	PUBLICITY £
7.77	13.20	2.99	20.00	42.96	2.59
8.00	3.95	2.99	185.63	30.00	20.97
		.75	6.98	4.20	16.45
	340.76	27.63			
	3.99	4.00			
	46.02	8.48			
£15.77	£408.67	£53.07	£205.63	£77.16	£40.01

Total £800.31
Budget £900
Balance £99.69
Balance after royalties (writer £84.73, composer £14.96) nil

Claiming your space – some scenic features

When you are creating a stage or performance area it is important to see where the performance floor space begins and where it ends, and the arrangement of masking can define this area. In traditional theatre buildings, where the stage is raised or separated from the auditorium, the delineation is clear; however, you may want to use the floor area as a designed feature and an indicator of place or atmosphere, the marker for the environment of performance. Using a stage cloth, or floor cloth, can be a simple way of doing this. These are most often made of canvas and tacked down with **clout pins** (big-headed tacks which can be easily pulled up with a claw hammer), or taped with dance tape. You can also use **gaffer tape**, which is a less expensive, wide tape also used for taping cables to the floor and is the most useful piece of equipment for a touring company, as it is very strong, can be painted over and can be used for quick repairs. Another form of flooring frequently used is **dance floor**, which comes in different colours but mostly in white and black and is sometimes reversible. This is high quality **polyvinyl chloride** (PVC) flooring and is laid in widths, which is then secured with gaffer tape. It should not be walked on with shoes that may damage its surface. It can make a successful flooring, and if you have any old pieces, these can be painted to suit your design. You can, of course, lay a floor in wood, using planking or plywood, which you can paint with your desired pattern or effect. The feasibility of any of these materials will depend on how long you have to assemble the set. It is possible to make a false floor that comes in 8 feet × 4 feet segments made of ¾-inch plywood, over which you could put a thinner plywood finish or **veneer**. This technique uses grades of sheet material and, depending on the final finish, it is effective for presenting different types of planked surface. Once glued to the rough plywood floor, various tools can be used to suggest that the flooring is made up of separate planks. A router, for example, has various blade attachments and can cut channels in wood.

Behind the performance area you may want to create a visual image using light and this can be done most effectively using a cyclorama. This can be either cloth or plaster and is a white expanse which fills the back wall area and sometimes even curves around the stage space, though it is most often hung at the rear of the stage area. It requires to be stretched to give a smooth appearance by **cyclorama stretchers**, which are blocks of wood with **sash**, thin rope, attached to them and which enable the stretchers to be tied off to points along the back wall of the theatre. Stage curtains are known as **tabs** and **drapes**. The tabs run across the stage on a **tab track**, which is attached to a bar or fixed to the grid or ceiling of the venue and different curtains can be attached to the tab track with the correct fittings, known as **bobbins**. A full set of curtains can be flown in and then pulled open or shut as appropriate.

The range of three-dimensional objects that can be placed on stage is limitless and depends on the choices you make for any given production. **Rostra** are stage platforms that are collapsible, most types having folding frames known as **gate legs**, which support a top, but they can be built as more solid structures. In addition, you may design **ramps**, **stairs** and **trucks** – all of which will require attention to **joints** and **weight loading**, depending on what is going to be performed on them. The principles underlying the construction of these structures are the same, be they triangular or curved.

The arrangement of scenic elements can add another dimension to your performance space. Whether your structures indicate an architectural feature or whether they are more abstract, you need to have a clear idea of the effect you wish to create.

Dance

The creation of a performance which is either wholly dance or includes dance sequences requires a different approach in the rehearsal room to one taken from a written text. In the rehearsal room, the reference for such a work will come from the dancers and choreographer and director. In this form, as with any work that is created within the rehearsal space, while the need for clarity of communication is paramount, some miscommunications can often result in the most interesting sequence of ideas. The key in this kind of process is to be open to possibilities.

The two shows used as examples in this chapter differed in their method of creation. *The Secret of Life*, like the *Bed of Arrows* trilogy discussed in Chapter 4, used a story from the Mahabharata, developing a dance style which was contemporary, and using some classical Indian dance ideas of Kathkali. *The Magic Shoes* was a scripted text which had a number of set pieces of dance. *The Secret of Life* was performed twice at the Queen Elizabeth Hall in London and, later the same year, over four nights at The Place, also in London. *The Magic Shoes* toured middle-scale venues throughout England, with a capacity of between 250 and 1,000 seats.

Case Study

The Secret of Life produced by Akshaya Dance Company
- Queen Elizabeth Hall, London (1995)
- Directed and choreographed by Pushkala Gopal and Unnikrishnan
- Music and storytelling by Sushi Kristnamurthi
- Designer: Marsha Roddy
- Lighting: Christine White

The Text

The Secret of Life tells of the adventures of Kacha and his attempts to obtain the secret of life mantra from the great guru Shukra. A bitter battle rages between rival factions in the heavenly kingdom and the demonic world of Pataala. In desperation, Brihaspathi, the ministerial adviser in the heavenly kingdom, sends his son Kacha to the demonic world to try to obtain Shukra's much-guarded mantra. The performance begins with Kacha having won the affections of Shukra's daughter, Devayani. Chatunni, Shukra's principal disciple, is incensed that Kacha is so popular and plots to get rid of him, hoping instead that he will become Shukra's son-in-law and heir to the mantra.

Vista stages

So-called for the views created behind the actor. These scenes owed a great deal to the ideas of perspective which Inigo Jones had used in the court masques, and Vista stages were put to great effect by playwrights such as Dion Boucicault (1820–90). These stage images were made possible by the development of theatre lighting and the work of stage designers such as Philippe Jacques de Loutherbourg (1740–1812), who was brought to London in 1771 by David Garrick (1717–79), the noted actor-manager of Drury Lane, London.

Technical Challenges

The production had a small budget and it was necessary to get-in and fit-up in one day and perform the next. The design solutions for this show needed to be fluid, simple and effective. The designer and lighting designer were free to decide on the stage setting and how it should develop. The tree of life, a potent symbol in the story, became the main feature of the stage set. The tree was made of paper rope and hung from the grid. Three static **gauzes** were used, as there were no flying facilities at the Queen Elizabeth Hall. Gauzes come in various gauges, and the number of holes and the width between each can alter the kind of effect that may be achieved. The gauzes enabled us to transform the space and provide magical moments of revelation as the story unfolded. The ds (downstage) gauze was painted to depict an exterior wall in an Indian village, with a doorway cut into it, leading to the school house. By strongly lighting the gauze from behind, what had appeared to be a solid feature became transparent, allowing the audience to see inside. The depth of the stage area at Queen Elizabeth Hall allowed us to put the tree of life far upstage. This meant that the tree and the performance in that area appeared through the downstage gauzes and gave the scene an ethereal quality. This depth of stage space is similar to the **Vista stages** of the eighteenth and nineteenth centuries.

A canvas floor cloth was painted to look like a sandy dirt floor. There are many ways of covering a stage floor but the floor cloth is the most easy to lay. It needs to be made of strong cotton duck, a plain weave cotton of 8 oz, 10 oz, or 12 oz should be strong enough to cope with wear and tear. When making a floor cloth the widths are sewn together so that the seams are parallel to the proscenium opening or the front edge of the stage space. They are sewn with the selvage edges face to face, then sewn to the canvas on the back, on the extreme edges of the selvage edge to produce a lap seam. When the cloth is laid these seams are usually directed downstage. This way the seams are less obvious to the audience. The outside edges are hemmed or have webbing stitched to the back around the edges of the cloth. The floor cloth is tacked or taped into place to stop it moving (see p. 83). There are no set dimensions for floor cloths as almost every stage or space is different in size.

As trees featured in the performance, it was very important to use tree gobos within the gauze area which gave an ethereal and wooded quality to the darker moments of the story. We also used a glass gobo which had a full moon etched on it; this was projected onto a black cloth at the rear of the stage. The glass allows a clear projected image, so the moon surface was seen with swirls and patterns, which gave an eerie effect. A fleecy cloud

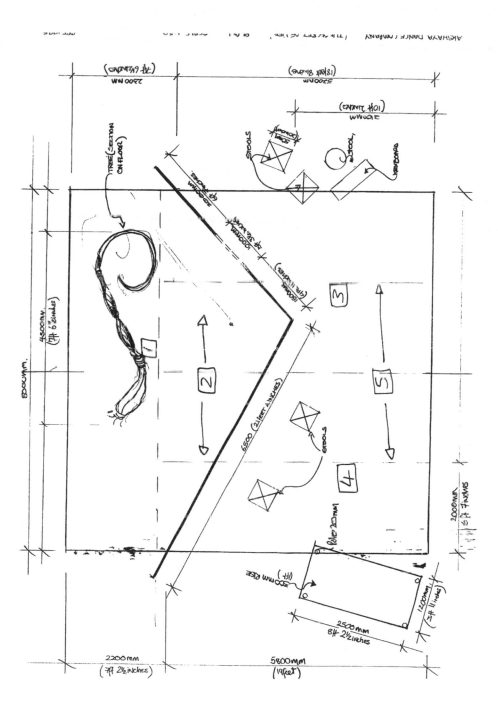

Figure 7.1 The set plan of gauzes for *The Secret of Life*, showing the five scene positions. The gauzes are at an angle, creating the impression of a solid wall.

effect was created with another projection. A special effect unit was used which works as a moving image. This image was also painted on glass and a motor moved the glass in front of the unit's beam of light. The motors can be speeded up or slowed down, so we had a choice of a fairly violent wind blowing or a rather more sedate passing of the clouds.

The gauzes formed a V shape instead of the more usual arrangement of hanging parallel to the front of the playing space. Light had to point at the gauzes flat on and therefore on both sides of the V shape in order to make the gauze opaque and show the painted bricks of the school house. If this failed to happen uniformly, the illusion of the brick wall would have been lost. Both of the gauzes which made up the V shape were drawn back on a tab track in Act 2. Above the stage was rigged a **drop box**. This box is usually rectangular and can hold light objects, for example a roll of cloth or petals. When a line is pulled the pin holding the lid closed drops out and so the contents of the box empty onto the floor. The drop box in this production contained lotus petals and pieces of material cut into the shape of lotus leaves, which fell to the floor at the appropriate moment.

There needs to be a thorough understanding of the stage space in a show such as this, so that the designers and director are always aware where the dancers will be at various parts of the music. The fact that there was no written score for the work added to the complexity of staging the production. Storytelling was used, which is often an improvised form, with voice rhythms and improvised set pieces. This meant that the music plot read like this: '5x2 =10bt rif – v/v + 2nd vocal + 1st vocal improvised – perky percussion – mrid + tabla here – ends with percussion arudhi.' Roughly translated, this means that part of the music should be in a 10-beat riff, the singer and second vocal part sing. The first vocal is improvised over the top. The note to percussion for this impro-visation is that it should be perky. Then the mirinda and tabla join in. The whole piece should end with percussion on the arudhi. The dance plot simply indicated 'K & D walk in', referring to Kacha and Devayani. The scenes were broken down into positions on the stage plan:

Position 1, upstage by the tree;
Position 2, downstage behind the gauze;
Position 3, stage left in front of the gauze;
Position 4, stage right in front of the gauze;
Position 5, downstage in front of the gauze.

So the scene breakdowns began to read like this: 'Scene 1 D & C [Devayani and Chatunni] dance at 1, cloth and respect ritual; to door in gauze, through door and come downstage, upstage lights fade; K [Kacha] enters stage left; Guru enters upstage behind gauze ... Enters through door to position 3 (this should always be the classroom).' As you can see, this notation is complex and needs to be cross-referenced with what you actually see in rehearsal and what you hear from the music. In order to give a sense of time distance we used smoke and light so that the guru appeared seemingly from nowhere, out of smoke. As this was so far upstage, the illusion worked very well.

Case Study

The Magic Shoes by Nona Shepphard
- The Playhouse, Whitley Bay, Northumbria (1994)
- Director: Nona Shepphard
- Choreographer: Jeanefer Jean-Charles
- Composer: Andy Dodge
- Designer: Marsha Roddy
- Lighting: Christine White

Technical Challenges

The Magic Shoes had to switch between two worlds: the real world, called The Patch, on Christmas Eve; and a fantasy world, called Shoeshine, on a similar festive occasion. Each of these places needed a different quality of light. The fantasy world, contrasting strongly with the real world, had to be lit in such a way as to focus on the characters' feet, because dance was the language of communication in Shoeshine. The costumes for this produc- tion also needed to be indicative of this world, with interesting shoes and shoe motifs. For example, the hats which were designed for the characters from this world were made in the shape and styles of shoes. These shoes on the performers' heads gave the audience the sense that they did not quite know which way up anyone was supposed to be. The costumes had to be flexible to perform in and designed to extend the expression and movement of the dance, and the fabric used was a synthetic viscose mix, because synthetic fabrics hold pleats much better than natural fibres. It was important that the style of the costumes was gender-free.

It was essential that the set design left as much of the stage space as clear as possi- ble for the dancers, and because the set was minimal, the objects which were chosen had a greater resonance than items in a traditional set. At the end of the piece both worlds collide and merge. The set design needed to give a sense of this composite feel. In dance it is always likely that the design will need to be precise, minimal and effective. Dance usually requires a conceptual and sculptural approach both for costume and lighting. Ideas have to be clearly expressed, even during rapid changes in time and motion both of performer, scene and sequence of action.

The changes of location were created with trucks. There was a bed truck for The Patch, which when turned around would reveal a fountain in the main square of Shoeshine. Another truck for The Patch was used for a graffiti-covered alley, and the reverse formed the arches of the royal palace in Shoeshine; an additional truck with a throne joined this, and its reverse was the end of The Patch's alley. A final truck was used for the prison in Shoeshine. This was a large boot which opened out to become a May pole, where a dance competition was held. The performance space was backed by a white cyclo- rama cloth behind a white **shark's tooth gauze**, on which was painted a skyline of rooftops and telephone wires. This urban skyline for The Patch disappeared in the land of Shoeshine by lighting the cyclorama in strong saturated colours.

Shark's tooth gauze

Shark's tooth gauze is most often used when transformations with light are called for. The principle of this effect is to light the gauze from the front and above at an angle of roughly 45 degrees. The light then 'fills' the gaps in the gauze and gives it a sense of solidity. Once the light is removed from this angle and light is used behind the gauze, the gauze becomes transparent. By playing with the balance of light from behind the gauze and in front of it, you can produce interesting effects, where you can see both in front and behind.

Aesthetics of light

The need for light came with a move to indoor theatre spaces and indoor performances such as those undertaken at court in seventeenth-century England. Up until this time performances took place in the open air and light sources such as candles or flaming torches would have been emblematic, used to indicate night or indicative of hell. The influence of light on acting styles over the centuries is often neglected. In dance we often find that the use of music, movement and light work as allied arts. Adolphe Appia (1862–1928) had an enormous impact on these theatre arts. With Émile Jaques-Dalcroze (1865–1951), the Swiss composer, Appia developed ideas of rhythmic spaces and Jaques-Dalcroze went on to create his system of eurhythmics, which was a precursor of contemporary dance as practised by Martha Graham (1894–1991) and Dame Marie Rambert (1888–1982). For Appia, the creative light was a light that interpreted and expressed the inner rhythmic movement of the drama and its musicality.

The development of lighting technology has enabled this sense of musicality to be further enhanced. The developments of dimmers have increased the range of possible transitions in terms of the movement of light through changes of intensity. Sophisticated lighting equipment can fade on or off, using instruments not only as groups but also in isolation. Lighting in the theatrical space has responded to changes in the spaces of performance. Simultaneous stages, like those described with relation to *The Secret of Life*, can be made to work due to the directing of the lighting. Lighting can pick people out, place them in silhouette, and can therefore be used to effect simultaneous presentations of performers and space, suggesting a distance in real time. Scenes, representing different geographical locations, can be placed on the same stage, like the set in *The Magic Shoes*. Lighting can sculpt the images that are presented and effect a symbolic design. It works on a number of levels and can present a mood which will provoke a complementary or contradictory mood in the audience. Lighting can be garish, festive and indulgent, but it can also induce a feeling of apprehension.

Lighting Equipment

Theatre lanterns fall into seven categories, **flood**, **cyclorama flood**, **fresnel**, **prism**, or **pebble convex (pc)**, **parcan**, **profile** and **automated moving light**.

A flood lantern does exactly what its name implies – it floods light out of the front of the unit. The cyclorama flood has a scooped reflector to send light up from the floor or down from the bar, depending on where it is placed to light the cyclorama. On *The*

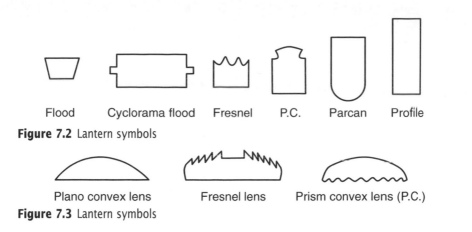

Flood   Cyclorama flood   Fresnel   P.C.   Parcan   Profile

Figure 7.2 Lantern symbols

Plano convex lens   Fresnel lens   Prism convex lens (P.C.)

Figure 7.3 Lantern symbols

Magic Shoes lighting plan in fig. 7.4 you can see floods on the bar. The fresnel has a ridged lens, and was first designed for lighthouses in order to make a large diffuse beam which could be seen from a long distance. You can recognise these lanterns by the stepped edges of the glass lens at the front of the lantern. These lanterns also have barn doors – flaps of metal which can be closed in on the beam to stop light spilling onto objects you do not want lit. The PC is a version of a fresnel, but with a smooth rounded lens at the front. This also creates a diffuse beam, due to the dimpled nature of the glass on the flat side of the lens, and these lanterns can also have barn doors. The parcan is a car headlight in a can. The par bulbs come with different fronts. These are **sealed beam** units, which means that the lens is attached to the reflector and the bulb. The most diffuse of the bulbs looks like a car headlight with criss-crosses on the glass and the narrowest beam is one where the glass is clear. There are grades in between these extremes. Whilst most lanterns give a circular beam, the parcan creates an elliptical shape. The bulb units were originally designed as aircraft landing lights. The profile is a spotlight which can profile an image or shape. This can be created by simply putting the shutters in on the lantern to make a shape or by using a gobo. Profiles can have two sets of plano convex lens, which allow them a greater range of size and definition. Any unwanted parts of a beam can be shuttered off. In addition, you can make the beam of a profile smaller by using an iris. You will need to focus to whatever shape you put in a profile.

Automated moving lights are the newest lantern technologies. They combine the features of the above lanterns with a programming facility. Thus, instead of manually focusing the light and moving barn doors, shutters or adding gobos, the automated light, or **intelligent light** as it is sometimes known, can be computer programmed to behave in particular ways. This means you can change the operation of these lights during the course of a production or simply plot them into a fixed position with colour and effect. These lanterns have motors and can be selected to **pan**, movement from left to right; **tilt**, up and down movement; **focus**, change beam size and definition they can also select gobos of which six or more patterns can be pre-rigged. In automated moving lights, colour change is achieved by means of a dichroic filter, which makes available

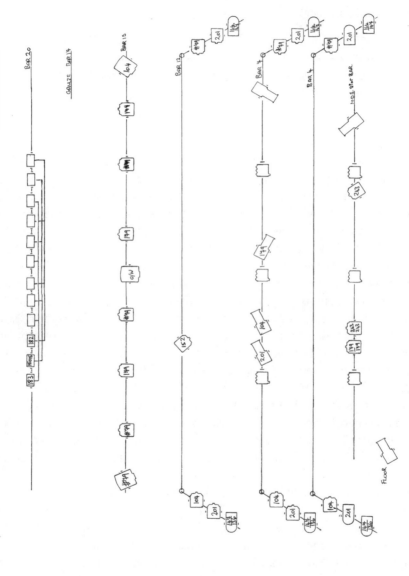

Figure 7.4 Lighting plan for *The Magic Shoes*. Note the symbols for different lighting units.

over 256 colours. Electric lantern technology for theatre is just over one hundred years old and the principles of lighting have been inherited from the earlier power sources of oil and gas. Automated moving lights have exploded that heritage and are likely to continue to develop in new and exciting ways.

The bulbs that are used in theatrical lighting equipment are generally **Tungsten Halogen**. They are described by both the metal filament and the gas that burns in the bulb; they are also described by the cap, the part that goes into the unit fitting. Some caps are **Eddison Screw** (ES), others are **Bayonet Cap** (BC). Many theatre bulbs, however, have more advanced caps, sometimes having two prongs, **bi-pin**, or having laps of metal, **flange screw**. The glass envelope that surrounds the filament and contains the gas is made of quartz, a very pure form of glass, which is able to withstand hotter temperatures without blowing the lamp. However, impurities left on the glass, such as greasy fingerprints will make that part of the bulb heat up to a higher temperature which will make the bulb blow more quickly. It is important, then to avoid handling the glass when changing a bulb. Lanterns are made up of a number of components: a lens, a reflector and a bulb. In order to focus a lantern one of these is moved in relation to the others.

Specific lighting terms, which refer to particular activities are used to plot a show and most are programmable through a computer board. You will often be working at a distance from the computer and an operator will activate your commands so it will avoid confusion if you learn this jargon:

Fade:	In or out, up or down. Either a **channel** or **circuit** or a group of channels to increase or decrease light or sound intensity.
Cross-fade:	To use two faders simultaneously, one bringing light up the other taking light out. Transferring smoothly from one **state** or light picture to another.
Snap:	An instantaneous operation, no time.
Full:	The maximum output which can be achieved.
Build:	To increase the apparent brightness of a state.
Add:	To bring additional circuits into an existing state.
Kill:	Remove from a state a single circuit, or a whole state; switch off.
Follow-on:	A second operation, which is part of the same cue, rather than becoming the next sequential cue.

Timings are given in seconds and can be programmed on computer boards.

Levels of light are graded on the faders from 0–10, or occasionally from 0–100.

There are a number of lantern manufacturers worldwide and each lantern has a symbol, which, when drawn on the lighting plan, denotes the lantern the designer wishes to use. There are generic symbols for lanterns and there are specific stencils for manufacturers' models. The most important aspect of your lighting practice is to identify the generic type of lantern that is required; in other words, which category from the list on p. 90 does the unit fall into? You must also identify the wattage you need either for your general illumination, or **general cover**, and for any special effects you wish to create

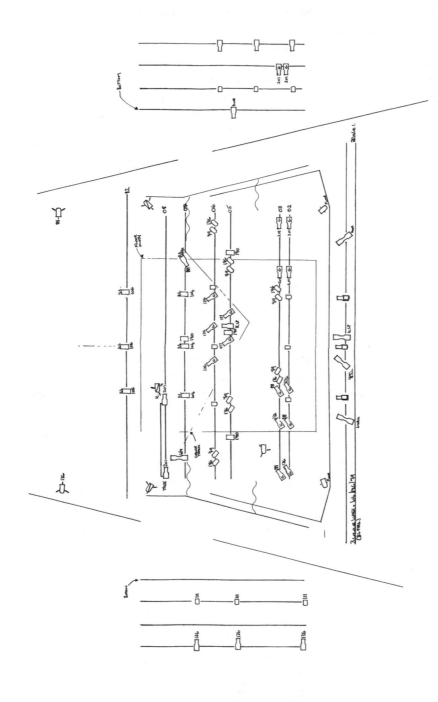

Figure 7.5 Lighting plan for *The Secret of Life*. Note the lantern symbols and key.

with light. By identifying the particular type of light required, it should be possible to check if it can deliver the overall artistic effect you wish to achieve.

Theory of Electricity: power to your performance space

The pressure which drives the current through a cable is measured in **volts** (V). The pressure in the UK is 240 V. The power required by an appliance is measured in **watts**. Some appliances require little electric power, such as a radio or a refrigerator, but others have a high power requirement, for example a large cooker requires 3,000–4,000 watts. The amount of current flowing through the circuit is measured in **amps**. As the power requirement is increased, so too is the amount of current flowing through the circuit. **Fuse** wire and fuse cartridges are measured in amps. The most useful equation for theatre electrics is: Watts ÷ volts = amps.

Voltage, current and resistance all have their equivalents in the water system. So a plumbing analogy is sometimes useful to explain the relationships in electricity. The factor that affects the flow of water is the diameter of the pipe. This forms a **resistance** against the flow of water. Resistance is a property of materials that reduces the flow of electricity through those materials. The higher the resistance, the more difficult it is for electricity to flow. The relationship of all these factors is known as **Ohm's Law**. There are two types of electricity, that which is produced by a battery, and that which is produced by a power station. The former is **direct current** (DC); the latter is **alternating current** (AC). There is a distribution point near your home. At each of these a transformer is linked to huge pylons which carry electricity across the countryside. Pylons support power lines which carry vast amounts of electric current from the power stations, where the electricity is generated. Some power stations are hydroelectric – that is, they produce electricity by the flow of water – others are powered by nuclear fuel or coal or gas which produce electricity by heat.

Electrons move from an area having net negative charge to an area of net positive charge. If an electron gains or loses the right amount of energy, it can jump to the next orbit away from the nucleus. Electrons in the outermost orbits can be detached and once

---

Health & Safety – general rules

On entering a new theatre space make sure you know where the nearest emergency exit, fire alarm and fire extinguisher are located. Make yourself aware of the type of extinguisher that can be used on electrical equipment. Remember that fires can be started by overheating cables, appliances or plugs. Avoid placing lanterns too close to material such as cloths and tabs. Be aware when hanging such pieces that although lanterns may not be in use during the rigging, they may be turned on once you have left the space. Do not hang set pieces near such equipment or else de-rig the lanterns first. In a theatre with a number of departments contact the relevant member of staff to discuss what you plan to do. Never touch equipment if you are not trained to use it. If someone experiences an electric shock, switch off the power supply. Do not touch the victim while they are connected to the source; find non-conductive material to move the victim away from the source. Only then, administer first aid and call for the emergency services. At no point put yourself in danger.

Health & Safety – safety precautions

In the performance space during the get-in, fit-up and rigging of a show follow these safety precautions:

- Hard hats should be worn at all times
- Make sure access equipment is properly secured.
- Make sure your working area is well lit.
- Always fit a suitable bulb to your working light.
- Never use a light socket as a power source.
- Working lights must be safely secured.
- Theatre lanterns should not be used as working light.
- Before switching on working light, make sure there is no risk of it igniting the set.
- At the end of your working day make sure that working lights are extinguished and power cables are cabled up and unplugged.
- Be sure to report any faulty equipment to the technical staff. If you can see the colour coding on a cable, then it is dangerous and is in need of repair. If the cable does not look adequately supported by the cable clip inside the plug, it is in need of repair.

detached, they are known as free electrons. **Insulators** contain only a few free electrons; some insulating materials are cloth, wood, china, polystyrene. **Conductors** contain many free electrons, particularly metals; some conducting materials are brass, copper, water. The electrons bob about indiscriminately, but given the right circumstances, they will flow in one direction and this forms the electric current. Batteries are made up of cardboard wrapping around a metal container called a **cell**, a soft jelly-like substance round a black sticky powder. These are chemicals to help electricity flow. Many batteries have a brass top and a long rod made of carbon running through them.

Amp, Volt, Watt and Fuse

Amp: ampere, basic unit of electric current; named after André Marie Ampère (1775–1836), French physicist and mathematician. **Volt**: unit of electromotive force; named after Count Alessandro Volta (1745–1827), Italian physicist best-known for the voltaic pile or electrochemical battery (1800), the first device to produce a continuous electric current. **Watt**: unit of power expended when 1 ampere of direct current flows through a resistance of 1 Ohm; named after James Watt (1736–1819), Scottish engineer and inventor. **Fuse**: a protective device to safeguard electric currents, containing wire that melts and breaks the circuit when the current exceeds a certain value. The fuses in a consumer unit protect the lighting circuits and act as a back-up protection for other circuits. Before the electricity reaches the consumer it will pass through a series of rewirable fuses or cartridge fuses, or in more modern homes, a **trip switch** or **circuit breaker**.

Your knowledge of how electricity works will now inform your work in lighting and sound. Both these areas require knowledge of how to calculate the number of lanterns you can use per circuit in a theatre, and in sound this knowledge will help you understand the nature of watts per channel of sound and the use of microphones. It is important to have a basic understanding of how electricity works in order that you understand the way in which light can be moderated. The units of operation are in fact very simple and many of the most efficacious effects have been made by a few lighting instruments thoughtfully placed, rather than a mass of equipment. A key feature of lighting design is to try and achieve your desired effect with a minium of equipment and to have thought carefully about the ways in which light casts shadow and illuminates, both physically and metaphorically.

RIGGING EXERCISE

Draw a plan using symbols for the lights you have in your performance space. Use the generic symbols for the lights. Find the lanterns you need for your bar and place them in the position, as shown on the plan, on the floor. Make sure each lantern has a **safety chain** which is fastened end to end. The chain is attached to the lantern and locked over the bar once the light has been rigged.

Find out from the plan how the bar is to be plugged up. It may be that the bar has sockets on it, which are called an **Internally Wired Bar** (IWB). If an IWB is used, the lanterns are plugged into the nearest socket and the plugs at the end of the bar are plugged into the numbers marked for each lantern on the plan. If you are not rigging on an IWB, you need to find out where the circuits are located in the theatre and how much **cable** you will need once the bar has been flown out in order to get them plugged in. (Electric cable runs the power supply to the light unit; it comes in a number of lengths and is graded for different levels of current.) Once you have done this, get the suitable lengths of cable and start with the lantern that is farthest from your power source.

Tape the socket to the bar with black PVC tape and plug in. Go to the next lantern, taking up the cable you have just used and tape it and your next socket to the bar and plug in your lantern. This procedure should be followed to the end of the bar and all your lanterns should be plugged to a cable. You must next check that all the rigged equipment is working and label each plug at the end of the bar with the circuit number it needs to be plugged into. To do this we use a **hot line**, which is a cable that can be plugged into 13 amp domestic sockets. This means you can plug in each cable individually and check the lantern and cable at the same time. Before hot-lining, shout a warning so that the crew knows what you are about to do. (When a lamp blows it occasionally makes a loud bang and no one should be standing directly in front of the lantern or have his or her face near it.) Once you have completed the rigging and the bar corresponds to the plan, and you have checked that it all works, you are ready to fly the bar out, or if you have been working on a fixed grid, you are ready to focus the lights.

ELECTRICAL EXERCISES

If power is measured in watts and is shown by the letter P, volts are shown by the letter V, and I represents amps which refers to the current, using the following possible equations see if you can answer the problem below:

$$\text{Ohm's Law:} \quad P = V \times I; \text{ or } I = \frac{P}{V}; \text{ or } V = \frac{P}{I}$$

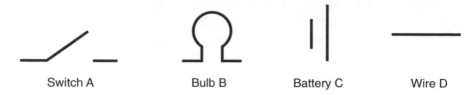

Switch A   Bulb B   Battery C   Wire D

Figure 7.6 Electricity symbols

- If a 1000 W heater has a supply of 240 V, how many amps does it draw?
  Answer, 4.16 amps. We therefore need to use a 5 amp fuse in this appliance.

- When theatre technicians and electricians design circuits they use the following symbols. A circuit is a complete unit. It should contain all these symbols if you are to make the light bulb work. You can use any amount of wire but what is important is the direction of flow of electricity which you indicate by placing an arrow on the line. Using all of the above symbols draw a simple circuit.
  Answer The circuit should have A – D – C – D – B – D – A

- A 2 kW electric fire is connected to a 240 V supply. What amp fuse would you need to place in the plug?
  Answer 10 amp.

- A 200 W television is connected to a 240 V supply. What amp fuse would this appliance require?
  Answer 0.83 Therefore, a 1 amp fuse.

- Using your electricity company's information chart, add up your consumption of electricity in your bedroom.

CHAPTER 8

Touring Opera and the Management of Sound

Case Study

The Secret Garden adapted from the novel by Frances Hodgson Burnett (1911)
- Warwick Arts Centre (1991)
- Composer: Helen Galvin
- Libretto: Nona Shepphard
- Director: Nona Shepphard
- Designer: Jenny Carey
- Lighting: Christine White

An adaptation of *The Secret Garden* by Frances Hodgson Burnett, the opera was commissioned by Theatre Centre and toured as a middle-scale production throughout England to a variety of venues. The Blackpool Grand (1,000 seats) was the largest venue; the smallest, the Theatre Royal, Margate, Kent (250 seats). While the seating capacity of a theatre does not necessarily indicate the size of the auditorium, it usually indicates the potential size of the playing space. Nevertheless, some large auditoriums can have relatively small stage areas. For example, the Hackney Empire, London, designed by Frank Matcham (1854–1920) in 1901, has an auditorium of over 1,000 seats but an average-sized proscenium arch stage 11.59 m wide by 9.75 m–12.2 m high (the height of the proscenium can be raised depending where the masking border is set). By comparison, the London Palladium, also built by Frank Matcham in 1910, has an auditorium capacity of 2,317 seats, with a proscenium arch stage 24.4 m wide by 12.5 m high. The Palladium is noted as one of the major United Kingdom venues for musicals and the stage is very wide indeed. Knowledge of the size of stage and auditorium is vital when considering the use of sound and, in particular, the reinforcement of sound by microphones to enhance the human voice or acoustic instruments.

Technical Challenges

Unlike a musical comprised of dialogue and song, opera has a continuous music structure. In *The Secret Garden* there were five musicians, playing an electric keyboard, tabla, sitar, cello, flute and African drums. Each had a microphone or an input which could be

Figure 8.1 A mixer showing input and output faders. Beside it, a reel-to-reel tape machine.

controlled via the **mixer** and balanced with the voices of the company. The mixer processes input signals, and can balance one volume against another. Any sound source goes into the **input** channel and is released to the loudspeakers via the **output** channel. Microphones are rarely used in the production of opera, but as electronic instruments are increasingly introduced to this art form it becomes necessary to use microphones to enhance voices, in order to balance the singing, electric instruments and acoustic instruments. However, the composer wanted the singing to sound as natural as possible, clear and unforced, avoiding the heavily produced sound that occurs in modern musicals. In musicals the balance of dialogue and song is paramount, as the performers switch between their speaking voice and their singing voice. Each production is different, but a general rule is to try to minimise the use of microphones for the speaking voice and to use microphones to enhance the singing voice. However, if the accompanying music tends to be noisy, the prominence of the microphones will largely depend on what makes the performer clearly audible.

Atmosphere, locale, text and sources

Sound, like lighting, is directional and needs to be thought about carefully if the audience is to receive the information you wish to convey. This is where an understanding of your performance environment is very important. Concave surfaces can focus sound and create echoes, while convex surfaces will disperse sound. In some concert halls acoustic baffles hang above the stage and auditorium to produce better acoustics in that space. For the same reason, most auditoriums try to avoid parallel walls and have walls which are slightly angled or surfaced with angled pieces or brick in order to stop the sound bouncing around quite so much. The seating arrangement will also affect how the sound behaves. Staggered seating enables the audience to hear more clearly as well as see more clearly, because the head of the person in one row is not in direct line with the person in the next and therefore does not interrupt the sound path. When touring a show to a number of differently shaped venues this balance becomes difficult to manage. It is extremely important for the sound designer to be able to use the mixer to **attenuate** the sound – that is, to manipulate the variable losses from the sound which are likely to occur.

Sound in theatre began with the use of live stage effects, usually required for battle scenes, which was discussed in Chapter 3. This type of effect is the most simple to control and very often the means of delivery for a sound effect – the means by which the audience hears it – is determined by the director's aesthetic choice. If the audience is to believe that a gunshot has occurred, there is no better way to achieve this than by taking a gun and shooting it, using blanks. The immediacy of the shot and, most importantly, the **decay** time, or the time it takes for the sound to subside, are enormously difficult to evoke in a recording. Similarly, crashes of crockery are best done live and if the text requires this action to be out of view, then a **crash box** of old bits of china and glass is the best way of providing this sound effect. In addition, the sound can be amplified by placing a microphone near the box and playing it back through the sound system. Door bells and telephone rings are also best done live, although a quality recording on a minidisc can provide a good alternative. The choice of whether to produce live sound or recorded sound will depend on whether the actor is to be integrated with the sound effect. For example, the performer must answer the phone after a certain number of rings if it is recorded; if it is live, then the actor picking up the phone will naturally interrupt the ring. This choice is dependent on the availability of a crew member to **cue** and operate the function. A cue is a signal that initiates a change; often a cue comes with a line of text spoken or a movement the actor makes, which becomes the **cue point**.

Taped and recorded effects come in a number of formats. There are reel-to-reel machines and tapes which run the tape from one spool to another, passing over a play head. This tape can be **edited** by cutting, or **splicing**. The tape can be interrupted with blank or coloured tape, **leader tape**, which separates the cues. Cassettes are more difficult to edit and so are best used to provide long periods of atmosphere. For example, in *The Secret Garden* sounds of the countryside were required to run for some time as a background to the performer's speech and singing. A cassette tape was an easy way of delivering that sound and each theatre we toured provided a cassette machine for playback though the mixer.

There are a number of ways of collecting sounds. Cassette tapes and compact discs (CDs) comprising collections of sound effects can be purchased, or you can record your own, which, in fact, can be more effective and original, but remember to listen to the recording on headphones as you do it. Unless you are in a very isolated area, beware of other noises such as passing cars or mobile phones, and so on – in other words, beware of anachronisms. In *The Secret Garden*, for example, such sounds would not have been appropriate for the period of the production.

Sound effects on commercial recordings, while convenient, will not produce highly textured sounds until they are processed through the mixer. The mixer can collect sound signals from various sources. These sources can be microphones, record decks, tape recorders, CD players and minidisc players. The mixer, if necessary, can amplify the source sound to what is known as **line level**. Through the mixer, the sound signals can be distributed to various destinations, such as amplifiers and loudspeakers, other tape recorders and processors. The mixer also permits the adjustment of tone quality, treble and bass frequencies, through an **equalisation** section.

The signal level that arrives at the mixer can vary considerably in strength and may be divided into two types: **microphone level**, or **mic** (pronounced 'mike') **level**, which is weak, and **line level**, which is generally strong. There is not one universal line level, it can be domestic, semiprofessional or professional. The semiprofessional line level may be found in small recording studios and the professional, with broadcast quality, is found in large studios. The signal level is measured in volts and the range is enormous, from 0.0001 V to 10 V, a factor of 1 million. Sound engineers prefer to work in voltage ratios which are determined by a logarithmic unit called a **decibel** (dB). Faders and meters on sound equipment are usually calibrated in dBs. A dB is not a unit of measurement but is used to describe how much a signal level has gone up or down. Most sound systems operate at one of the standard line levels. When a signal leaves the mixer at that standard level, its ratio to the level is 1:1. Therefore a rise or fall from that level will result in a different ratio, 2:1, 4:1. When the ratio is 1:1, it is described in dBs as 0 dB, as there has been no change from the standard level. Any rise or fall in the signal level away from the standard level will be referred to as + dB or – dB. Here are some examples:

If the voltage of the standard line level = 1 V then,
voltage dB   0 = +20
                            4 = +12
                            2 = +6
                            1 = 0dB
                        0.5 = –6
                      0.25 = –12
                    0.125 = –18
                        0.1 = –20
                  0.0625 = –24

A common standard line level is 0.775 V and dBs are measured above and below this point. This may sound rather complex but it is simply the units of change that are used on sound equipment and you will see these measurements on mixers.

Compact disc, minidisc and **digital audio tape** (DAT) are formats which can allow for more precise cueing. Generally, CD may be used for atmosphere rather than **spot cues**, or precise cues, due to the imprecision of the playback machines. Minidisc and DAT are modern methods of providing spot cues, such as an explosion, incidental music, cars starting, and the sound of footsteps. They have more precise playback machines and can be edited with the kind of precision that can be achieved with the reel-to-reel, or ¼-inch tape. If the budget will not stretch to these modern appliances, it is possible to use a compact disc recorded with separate cues and played in performance on a domestic CD player.

As with most areas of technical theatre, sound must be judged to be appropriate to your work. Excessive sound reproduction lacks finesse and smacks of incompetence or lack of dramatic sense. Your audience should not be overly aware of sound effects, unless they have been specifically pointed up or highlighted for a dramatic purpose. There must be a naturalness and subtle balance between sound and the rest of the production. For example, the simple act of closing or opening a door requires finesse in recording – is the character angry, happy, bold, leisurely, timid, or does he just close the door in a matter of fact way? The force with which the door handle is grasped, the degree of effort in turning the handle, the timing between the opening and shutting, all are done in different ways to match the mood of the action. When you are making recordings you must interpret from the dialogue and action.

This attention to detail is most important as sound effects in the theatre can be used to establish locale, time of year, day or night, and the weather. They can evoke atmosphere and provide a link to scenes. They can act as an emotional stimulus and they can reproduce physical happenings, such as cars arriving and babies crying. They can also give a sense of movement, which can be achieved by panning sound between the two tracks of stereo. This can be done either when you are recording the effects or during playback in performance. If you prerecord such movements, however, you then have a fixed effect which means that, if action and sound are to be synchronised, the actor must follow the sound, which is often difficult to carry off. On the other hand, if the sound is created during the performance, the operator can follow the action, which is always preferable.

The chain of sound

In the recording of work or in sound reinforcement, the equipment used will be dependent on what is available and the size of the budget. Where possible, try to plan the best use of equipment. A **microphone** is a means of providing sound and a speaker is the means of delivery. It is interesting that they are mechanically the reverse of each other. The microphone is a device which captures a signal and sends it to the mixer. Inside the microphone is a magnet. A magnetic field is produced and as sound waves move, so do the particles around the magnet. The microphone converts this into an electric signal or pulse which travels down a sound cable to the mixer. The loudspeaker has a magnet and a cone which vibrates as the signal is played through it. As all speech is simply the transmitting of sound waves, it can be described as a system of **frequencies**. Sounds which vibrate many times are known as high frequency and those which vibrate less frequently are known as low frequency. In the same way, musical instruments respond at different frequencies. The **pitch** of an African drum will be entirely different to that of a sitar. The pitch of a note is a combination of frequencies, which identify the position of that note on the musical scale.

The sound reinforcement required for the instruments in *The Secret Garden* had to cope with instruments and voices with very varied pitch, frequency and decay. The position of microphones and loudspeakers in relation to actors and audience will change the sound reception. Most sound designers agree that there is no substitute for listening carefully to what you are producing and reflecting on its effectiveness. Whilst there are mathematical formulae which can help determine the use of equipment, there is no better way to decide how to use sound than to listen to it.

Speakers can be rigged overhead on bars or they can be placed on the floor. If rigged overhead, they need to be securely locked off with a **G-clamp** and have at least one safety chain attached to them. When planning where to put your speakers you should try to get them equidistant, so that the audience receives a good all-round **sound picture**, that is, the sense of illusion created by the sound should be consistent with what the audience sees. If you want the audience to believe that a carriage has just pulled up at the front door, neither of which they can see, it is necessary to place a speaker in the vicinity of the front door, or where they believe it to be. It is also wise to remember when dealing with nature sound effects that birds are generally heard from above. Consider carefully the impression you wish your audience to receive.

From the 1930s to the 1960s sound reinforcement in Britain and the United States was limited. In theatre it was primarily used for musicals, where microphones would have been turned up for songs and turned down for speech. These productions used microphones along the front of the stage, known as **float mics**. In the past the downstage edge of the stage had been where footlights or floats had been positioned, so-called because the light was created by wicks floating in wax. This position is still used for lights and sound. Where possible, an odd number of microphones should be placed along the front of the stage, which will ensure that a microphone is always at the centre of the stage.

Microphones have particular pick-up patterns and need to be chosen and focused to achieve an even cover of sound collection. There are three basic patterns, **omni-directional**, **bi-directional** and **cardioid**. The omni-directional microphone collects sound from all around and is rather indiscriminate. The bi-directional microphone, as the name suggests, collects sound from two directions and its pattern is like a figure of eight, where the waist of the eight has least pick-up. This microphone is very good for interviews between two people. The cardioid microphone is heart-shaped, resulting in one side of the microphone having a very wide pick-up, whilst the other has nearly no response at all. These microphones are more directional and avoid collecting extraneous sound. During live mixing, the variety of microphones, instruments and acoustic spaces make it essential that sound operators hear the same sound quality as the audience and for this reason they should ideally be placed in the auditorium with the mixer and playback equipment. If this is not possible, which is often the case, the sound booth should have a removable window.

As soon as a number of sound sources are used, a mixer is required to control those sounds and direct them to the speakers in the auditorium. Speakers should be placed where they will give the clearest sound and where they reinforce the illusion that the sound is coming from the stage area. For special effects, speakers may, of course, be put anywhere in an auditorium, depending on where the sound should appear to come from. The best place for speakers is directly above the performance area and in the centre. They should be placed on the audience side of microphones to avoid **feedback**, which turns into a high-pitched whining and will occur if a microphone is picking up sound directly from a speaker. It goes through the speaker, back to the mixer and is once more picked up by the microphone. Hence, it is often known as **howl round** and will not cease until either component is moved and/or the fader is taken down on the mixer. Extra care should be taken when setting up microphones and speakers in a touring show, but feedback problems should be easily remedied as the sound designer becomes familiar with the space.

In the upstage positions for *The Secret Garden* it was important to rig **shotgun mics** or **rifle mics** as they are sometimes known. These microphones are highly directional and can pick up voice and instruments from an overhead position. **Radio mics** can be attached to the performer and are useful because they allow the performer complete freedom of movement on or off stage; the pick-up is extremely localised and so a clean sound is possible. However, radio mics are very expensive and were beyond the budget of *The Secret Garden*.

It was important when using live music for *The Secret Garden* that the performers and musicians could hear themselves. In order that the singers could hear the musicians properly, **foldback speakers** were placed on the floor in the wings and provided onstage sound. The sound operator can accentuate the singers' voices over the musicians in the mix of sound they send to these speakers.

There are a number of factors, then, to be considered in the management of sound. There are choices about sound reinforcement and sound production from prerecorded sources. A **sound plot** will help you to manage these features. The sound plot for *The Secret Garden* was based on live sound. For example, a sequence would have read something like this: African drum – mic; sitar – mic; tabla – mic; flute – mic; cello – mic, electric keyboard – DI box (**direct injection box**) The DI box can be used on all electronic instruments and sends the signal straight to the mixer. For *The Secret Garden* there were six inputs from the musicians to the mixer. In addition, there were three float mics at the front of the stage and two rifle mics above the stage. In total, eleven inputs, five of which had to be balanced to produce the singers voices at a consistent level anywhere on the stage. The sound plot changed at every venue and for every performance, as levels of sound are influenced not only by the architectural shape of the auditorium but also by how many seats are sold and how much clothing members of the audience are wearing. The impact of winter coats on sound levels can be quite staggering. Therefore, the sound operator works with the performers each night, monitoring and changing sound inputs and outputs as appropriate. For *The Secret Garden* this could be broken down into a central two-speaker set, auditorium left, auditorium right, and, in most venues, circle left and circle right, a total of six speakers, or outputs. Mixer desks are often described by the number of inputs and outputs. For this show we needed eleven inputs and six outputs. Mixers are made of modules for input and output and these come in pairs. This provides a right and left channel when using stereo equipment. For example, microphone channels use only one module input, whereas a CD input would use two modules because it has stereo sound. The minimum mixer requirement for *The Secret Garden* was 12–6. The two foldback speakers placed stage left and stage right were directed through the mixer **auxiliaries**, which are a means of sending the signal to other equipment; for example, an effects processor which could change the pitch, decay and sense of the sound. You can even process sound so that it appears to be in a much larger or smaller room. Some mixers will then have two further output faders which act as masters and control the mixer. At Oxford Playhouse, which was the second venue of the tour, the mixer specification was 24-8-2. If you add the reproduced sound to the show's requirement, an input for music playing from another source at the beginning of the show, a CD and a ¼-inch tape of spot cues, both of which required two faders each as they are stereo inputs, the sound

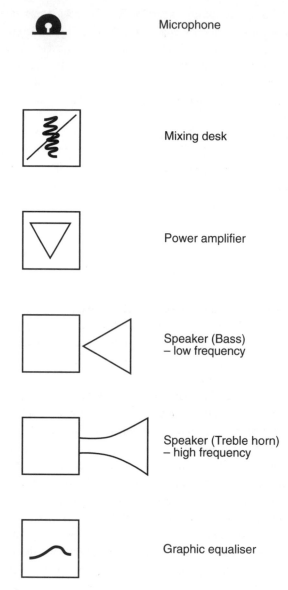

Microphone

Mixing desk

Power amplifier

Speaker (Bass)
– low frequency

Speaker (Treble horn)
– high frequency

Graphic equaliser

Figure 8.2 Sound system plan symbols

desk specification is actually 15–6–2. Oxford Playhouse had three **amplifiers** to power the speakers in the front of house.

The plotting of sound effects should be done as a **time line**. This will depend, however, on whether you are mixing together effects as you record them or are making a tape for theatre which you can play at the appropriate times within the performance. You may, for instance, wish to evoke a thirty-minute period of stormy weather. A sound effect for rain will be needed with spot cues for howls of wind. These howls must occur at particular moments in the performance, timed to the actor's movements and speech.

If they are prerecorded synchronisation with the actor will be extremely difficult. Hence two source machines will be needed: one which enables the rainy atmosphere to play and another for the operation of the spot cues. Then there may be the sound of the arrival of a carriage, the depositing of its occupant and its departing in the same direction as it came from. As the carriage leaves, the wind rises and dies out over one minute. This effect will require another source machine and tape in order for these fades to occur – one fading in and out over the other. The thirty-minute period could be plotted like this:

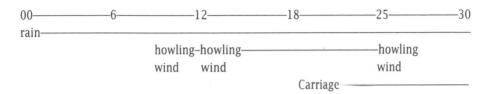

If you are making up the complete sound tape, the plot is a way of describing the recording. It shows where in the time frame the effects begin.

The timing of sound cues is intensely important and we have mostly concentrated in this chapter on the means by which sounds are recorded. Sound design, like all other areas of technical theatre, needs to be a part of a coherent sense of the performance piece. In this chapter we have looked at the practicalities, but you must also consider the aesthetic changes that can be created by a continuous soundtrack of a mixture of sounds and particular effects. Sound can potently direct your audience to the world you wish them to engage with.

SOUND EXERCISE

1   Using the symbols shown in fig. 8.2 draw a simple diagram to show the route by which a performer's voice might travel to a loudspeaker.
     Microphone
     Amplifier
     Equaliser
     Mixer
     Loudspeaker
2   Using a theatre and auditorium arrangement you know, draw a plan of speaker positions which will produce the cleanest sound.
3   Draw a diagram of your source machines and mixer which will achieve the following effects:
     • A carriage entering upstage right and stopping upstage left.
     • Dogs barking centre-stage.
     • Birds singing throughout the auditorium.
     • A space ship landing downstage centre.
     • An actor screams and is heard to echo throughout the auditorium.
     Plot which pieces of equipment would be best used for each effect.

4   The sound effects in question 3 must be placed on the following equipment:
  • on ¼-inch tape
  • on the same ¼-inch tape as above
  • on cassette tape
  • on minidisc
  • live

Record these effects on the above equipment or solve this sound plot with the equipment at your disposal.

CHAPTER 9

Spectacle

Case Study

You're Thinking About Doughnuts, adapted from Michael Rosen's story by Nona Shepphard
- Nottingham Playhouse (1996)
- Director: Nona Shepphard
- Designer: Marsha Roddy
- Lighting: Christine White

The Text

You're Thinking About Doughnuts was produced by Nottingham Playhouse and performed in the theatre's auditorium. It tells the story of Frank, a young boy who goes to the museum where his mother is a cleaner. Waiting for her to finish work, he gets the fright of his life when a skeleton comes to life and jumps out of its case. And so the adventure begins – the boy and the skeleton encounter many museum exhibits and their environments, including a moonscape, a tiger shoot in India, a room full of puppets and dolls, an eighteenth-century pickle factory, a Pop Art exhibit with Elvis Presley and Marilyn Monroe, who come to life, a witch's ducking stool, and statues of Greek gods, which also come to life and behave like a gang of yobs. There was also a 4.5-metre ebony statue of Tanganyikan man.

Technical Challenges

This show had major challenges for every department in the theatre. Wardrobe and prop-making between them had to create statues which come to life and a skeleton costume, which had to be comfortable and flexible, while appearing bone like and stiff, for this character never left the stage. Wardrobe had also to make a dress, 7 metres long, for the villainous Mrs Longstone, who worked in the museum and appears in a surreal sequence (see cover). In order to put the costume on, the actor had to climb to the top of a tallescope, which was draped with the skirt. The prop-making and construction departments made the ebony statue; the pitted surface of a huge full moon, which was trucked on; a large Fly which was flown in, huge 5-metre puppets which leaned against the entrance to the toy factory. There were also enormous flying pieces for the museum frontage and walls, and large trucks were wheeled on to make the pickle factory. The witch's ducking stool had to be in working order, as Frank was raised and lowered on it, listening in terror to a sound tape of a fifteenth-century mob killing a woman in this barbaric way. The sound department also researched with the director a large number of classic pieces of music that became an aural exhibit in itself.

This production had a large number of flying pieces, as we had to move quickly from one environment to another, as well as mechanical operations for the ducking stool, and the movement of the moonscape and the pickle vats on trucks. The movement of actors and settings were choreographed to facilitate these rapid changes of scene. The plot was fast moving and we felt that bringing in the house curtains or tabs to hide the scene changes would have interrupted the flow of the performance and reduced the dramatic tension. The quickest and most spectacular method by which scenes can be changed is by using flying systems. The majority of the bars for *You're Thinking About Doughnuts* were used to fly set pieces, some of which joined up to trucks to complete a scenic image. All the scene changes took place in front of the audience and were timed to pieces of music.

The cueing of lights, sound, flying, trucks and actors was a complex job for the deputy stage manager.

The Fly in *Doughnuts* was operated on a spot line, and the voice of the Fly was played by an actor speaking into a microphone in the wings. As the Fly spoke, the flyman operated the lines to the Fly to make it move, thus maintaining the illusion of a living insect. When flats are flown into position from above they are known as **french flats**. The museum flats and the museum doors were flown as french flats, using the counterweight system. You can see from the **flying plot** on p. 115 that these scenic pieces had to cross a number of bars so that their weight could be supported and easily flown in and out at speed.

Many theatres have a counterweight system, of which there are two types, double purchase and single purchase. However, the principle of operation is the same in each: the weights counter and balance the weight of the object to be flown. The flyman will add weights to the cradle in order to balance the weight of the object to be attached. These weights can be added while the floor crew starts to attach the object. For example, if you want to attach a flat to a bar, then you must attach **flying irons** to the flat in order that steel cables can be attached to the back of the flat. The rings and guides enable the flat to stand up and the steel cables can then be attached to the bar. Generally, bars or pipes hang from all the flying lines of a counterweight system and these can be raised and

Health & Safety

There are a number of ways of hanging things for the stage. Often this is called **flying**. Flying can be done by a number of systems, counterweights, winch bars, hemp, or from a grid on **spot lines**, which are dropped from the grid over pulleys to fly particular objects which only need one line because they are light in weight. For example, a small chandelier or a mosquito net might be flown in this way. If you are flying objects without the traditional theatre equipment, then you must bear in mind the weight of the object, as this will determine the necessary method. To use the example of the mosquito net again – it could be flown on fishing line of the correct strength. The outer frame of a doorway may also be attached to flying bars in the same way, providing the correct weight is selected for the line strength. It is important to ensure that a line has a brake on it before loading with weights or before attaching an object to the bar or lines at the other end. Never undo a brake on a counterweight unless you are sure you have the right bar and that it has been correctly weighted. It is essential during any work where people are above floor height that the rest of the team are wearing hard hats, and that one person is taking charge of the instructions from the floor, to the fly floor and to the grid.

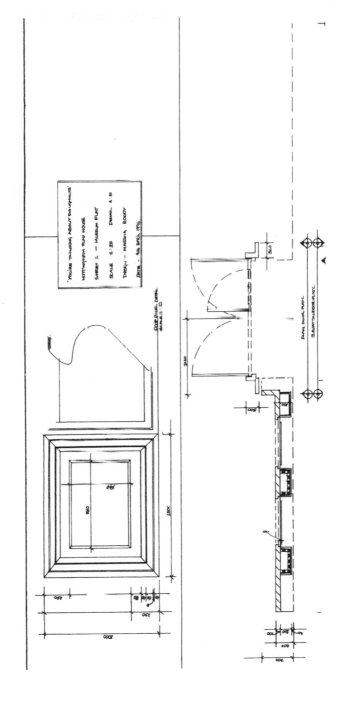

Figure 9.1 Section drawing of the museum flats as french flats in *You're Thinking About Doughnuts.*

lowered to change the position of the objects being flown. The cradle has a hemp line which runs up to a **clew**, an attachment which has steel lines running from it. These lines run over pulleys in the grid and drop down to the bar usually on stage left, stage right and centre stage, and are known as long, mid and short, depending on which side of the stage the fly rail is on and the length of each line from that point. The weighting of the cradle should err on the side of the cradle, given that it is heavier than the bar weight. This means that should the brake be inadvertently off, or should the flyman lose grip on a piece of set, the cradle will naturally take the object out towards the grid and not down towards the stage. To operate the system a brake is carefully released which will allow the rope to travel – upwards towards the grid and downwards towards the stage floor.

Another method of flying is by **hemp sets**. The principle of lines from the bar is the same but this time the lines come to the fly rail and are pulled manually. This means that all the weight of the object has to be pulled and very often requires a lot of people on the fly floor. This is especially true if the bar contains lighting units or sound speakers. The hemp rope goes over pulleys in the same way as in the counterweight systems; however, rather than running to a system of weights, they are cleated to the wall of the theatre. Each line pulls up a particular area on the bar – usually one in the centre, one stage left, another stage right of the bar. In order to level the bar, each line has to be altered individually, using the terms short, mid, and long to describe each line. The ropes are then tied off in a figure of eight around the cleat, with an inverted loop to finish. When loaded, one of these bars should be operated by a minimum of two people on the ropes. A knowledge of knots is essential in this operation. The clove hitch is a good holding knot and the bowline is most often used to tie onto an awkward object. It grips objects which have no obvious point to attach a rope to, such as a pole. An ordinary knot would simply slip along the length of the pole. The tie off, or lash knot, which is used for cleating flats together in a row, is also very useful. It is a quick release knot, which is useful for special effects and for passing equipment or objects to others when rigging (see fig. 4.1).

Winch bars, like counterweights, take the strain out of flying, but they cannot fly objects to cue and so are rarely used as part of the scenic movement during a performance. Some winch bars are ratchet winches which will stop when you stop winding; others have a metal brake and it is occasionally necessary to take the handle off and set it against the winch once the flying is completed, this then acts as an extra brake. Winch bars are often used for flying electrical and lighting equipment, as they take the strain of the load and do not require reloading. All flying must be done under supervision with one person on stage at all times watching the bars coming in and going out. This person should be giving instructions in order that bars and equipment do not snag on cable, curtains or set. One person only should be in charge of giving instructions as to the height of the bars and objects. These heights are then marked so that if they are moved or are to fly in on cue, the same position can be found again. These marks are known as **deads**, and are usually strips of coloured PVC tape which are wrapped around the rope. A piece of matching tape is placed on the rope which runs behind. When these two pieces of tape are in alignment, the in or out position for the piece of scenery is reached. These deads should be set before the technical rehearsal and then adjusted if necessary.

Flying people must be undertaken by specialist companies which set up the correct loading and apparatus by which an actor may be pulled into position. Kirby is the best-known company which make these systems. The various Peter Pans around the country often require its harness fittings, which are worn beneath the costume. The actor is attached to a line that runs both vertically and horizontally, and may be required to fly in on objects such as thrones and platforms. As these structures become heavier, so the method by which they descend needs to be more secure and very often motors are used which are attached to chain hoists.

Practical preparations for rehearsals

In the productions I have discussed in earlier chapters I have concentrated on different aspects of technical theatre. The key to all these areas is stage management. A wide variety of stage management takes place in the production of a piece of spectacle theatre which must be precisely co-ordinated. The first part of these preparations occurs in the rehearsal room, where the ground plan is marked out on the floor and is used for reference by all the theatre departments.

The ground plan is paramount for the working through and solving of any problems which may arise as the rehearsal and production process develop. At the get-in and fit-up of the production the stage will be marked out by stage management. The lights and sound equipment is then rigged and the scenic features are brought in, constructed and assembled.

In the rehearsal room and on the stage it is necessary to be clear where the onstage and offstage positions are, so the **mark-out** is made with PVC tape on the floor. At the beginning of the rehearsal period, when the team is working from a text, a design may already have been completed. Usually in the first week of a production the actors and all technical and design staff will see the model, costume drawings and stage plan. The mark-out on the rehearsal floor must indicate entrances and exits and other features of a set such as stairs or windows. During the devising process it is wise to add features to the mark-out as they are decided upon, as scenic elements not only change what is possible in rehearsal but also give a real-time feeling of what the performance area will be like. For example, an indication of how long it takes to cross from the door to the window will be crucial for the actors, directors and designers.

In the set fit-up, all major scenic elements and structures must be set up, and lights and sound equipment rigged, before the lighting design is followed and the lights focused. The fit-up is carried out with reference to the ground plan and the stage is often marked out in the same way as the mark-out in the rehearsal room. Prior to and during the weeks of production the set designer will have presented a series of drawings and pictographic impressions of the effects he or she wants to achieve. A scale model of the final set, scale plans and **side elevations** of major scenic items will also have been drawn for the technical departments. Side elevations show a cross-section of an object or stage space. This is a most useful diagram for looking at the heights of constructed elements in the stage space. The ground plan will include every detail of the setting. For example, in shows like *You're Thinking About Doughnuts* all flying pieces will be identified and drawn to scale.

When designing and preparing the plan, attention must be given to gangways, health and safety, backstage access and storage space. The set designer will liaise with the

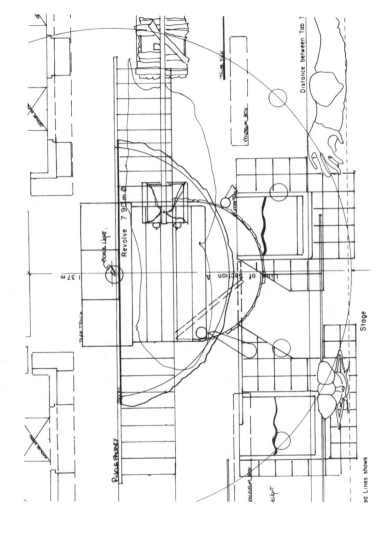

Figure 9.2 Ground plan for *You're Thinking About Doughnuts*, showing the sightline angles.

production manager to ensure that all these areas are considered. In addition, the angles of viewing and blind spots, or sight lines, will be taken into consideration. Care must be taken that the audience can see actors on all levels of the stage from any seat in the auditorium.

As you can see from the ground plan in fig. 9.2, the majority of scenic pieces for *Doughnuts* were flown. The flying plot – the list of objects and pieces to fly and the bars on which they fly – was as follows:

Bar 1	The Fly
Bar 2	Big Puppet
Bar 3	Masking border
Bar 4	Lighting bar
Bar 5	Pickle (factory) lights
Bar 6	Lighting bar
Bar 7	Free
Bar 8	Museum boxes (illuminated display cases containing fish and birds)
Bar 9	Tiger silks
Bar 10	Masking border, with a spot line for pickle factory spoon
Bars 11–15	River
Bar 16	Border, with a spot line for a single pickle factory light
Bar 17	Lighting bar
Bar 18	Free
Bars 19–21	Museum windows
Bar 22	Museum doors
Bar 23	Tiger silks
Bar 24	Masking border
Bar 25	Science box sign (illuminated museum sign)
Bar 26	Free
Bar 27	Lighting bar
Bars 28–31	Free
Bar 32	Blacks

The scenes of the show broke down into the exterior of the museum, the inside hall of the museum, the moonscape, the Tiger exhibit, the Fly scene, the toy collection, the Marilyn and Elvis scene, the ducking stool, the pickle factory. There is usually a stage manager in rehearsals from the very beginning of the process of production. In most large theatres it is the Deputy Stage Manager who attends rehearsals and it is this person who will be responsible for cueing the show in performance from a prompt copy, now more commonly called **the book**, which contains the blocking from the rehearsal, all the cuts in the script, and production notes and details of discussions and meetings, places for sound, and lighting and special effects cues which have been finalised in the technical rehearsal. In other words, the prompt copy is the master copy of the script or music score, containing all the actors' moves and the technical cues. It is used by stage management to control and run the show.

All notes in the prompt copy are pencilled in during rehearsal. After the final rehearsal and before the performance the DSM should ink in the cues and standby points for the cues, sometimes-colour coding by department, with standby calls in red and the cue points in green. The golden rule, however, is that the chosen format must be clear should anyone take over if the DSM is unable to do the job. From each GO a line should be drawn to the appropriate point in the script. See the prompt copy from *You're Thinking About Doughnuts* in fig. 9.3; note the blocking and other comments made on the facing page.

The Assistant Stage Manager is often responsible for marking out the rehearsal space to the correct layout of the set design and the preparation of a props list from the text. After confirmation with the director and the designer, the ASM will commence the job of acquiring the props for the production. The list changes each day of the rehearsal, expanding or contracting, as the DSM updates the ASM on decisions taken. A sample from the props list drawn up for *You're Thinking About Doughnuts* follows:

SCENE 1
Mop and bucket
Duster
Packet of crisps (personal to Frank)
Handkerchief (personal to Frank)

SCENE 4
3 × clubs for gods
2 × swords for gods
1 × javelin for gods.

Working with the director, the DSM draws up a **call sheet** at the end of each day's rehearsal, which is a list of the actors who are required to attend the different rehearsals. It is the DSM's responsibility to ensure that actors know their **calls** for the following day's work. For example, this is one day's call sheet for *You're Thinking About Doughnuts*:

CALL SHEET
NAME	TIME
David Lemkin	9.00–10.00
Lyn Christine	9.00–10.00

    To rehearse Marilyn and Elvis

To Join:
Marc Joy
Rashan Stone
Shobna Gulati   } 11.00–13.00
David Hudson
Dawn Wrench
Dale Superville

    To rehearse Stonemen and opening sequence

FULL COMPANY   14.00–18.00
    To rehearse the Pickle Factory

Some directors do not use a calls system, however, preferring the performers to attend each day to work together in an **ensemble** fashion. This arrangement allows greater flexibility and with a small cast can result in inventive rehearsal work. Directors who have planned their rehearsals on a calls basis wish only to have the relevant performers in the rehearsal room.

Rehearsal notes, an extensive list of detailed notes of the day's rehearsal and its implications for technical departments, are delivered each day to all departments. An example from a *Doughnuts* rehearsal illustrates the need for **running props** – props which in the course of a production need to be replenished.

	Mr Longstone We've got the glass cases.
	Skeleton Run, Frank . . .
	Mrs Longstone We decide what goes in the glass cases
LX Q 68 (light up stonemen in arches)	Mr Longstone This is MY museum.
Smoke Q 8 (Fawcett enters)	The lights are changing. Through the windows we see the Stonemen coming to life. – General Fawcett charges in.
LX Q 69 (X finds and lose Pickle Lights) Truck Q 4 (Pickle truck vat opens)	Fawcett This is my museum. Forward men!
Fly Q 28 (Pickle factory flat out)	Stonemen We are the heroes, we are the heroes.
Sound Q 72 (Young Persons Guide to the Orchestra)	The back walls fly out. The stonemen are in!
Company clear pickle tables. Frank jumps into Pickle vat with Mum in jar. Fly Q 29 (Pickle lights fly out)	Longstones Get them!!!
FO Pickle truck exists s.r. Sound Q 7 a (fade down) FX – Gunshot	It is pandemonium. General Fawcett sees Tiger. Fawcett Aha! My bag!
	He shoots at Tiger and chases her.
	Stonemen Biff 'em, clunk 'em, biff 'em.
Sound Q 73 (fade to top level) LX Q 70 (lose light on African statue) Visual as Stonemen pick it up.	The Stonemen have medals on. The African figure is there. They start to pick it up to use as a battering ram again. The women are dismantling the factory and throwing pickles

Figure 9.3 Prompt copy for *You're Thinking About Doughnuts* with a sketch for Bryman's pickle factory.

No. 10

Copies to: Director, Designer, Lighting Designer, Sound Designer, Chief LX [electrician], Stage Manager, Technical Manager, Deputy Technical Manager, wardrobe, props, paintshop, Associate Director, SM office, Construction Manager, publicity, Production Manager, Theatre Director's office.

NOTES

All Departments
1 Please note there will be a progress meeting at 9.30 a.m. on Thursday in the green room [backstage room where performers rest or receive visitors].

Stage Management
1 Please note that Lyn Christine requires a handbag (see Marsha, as she may choose one from wardrobe).
2 Please note, Friday lunch time will be fine for the props spread.
3 Please note the following props for the Pickle Factory:
   a. cauliflowers and carrots to chop.
   b. a knife to chop the carrots, etc.
   c. a ladle to scoop the pickle into the bucket (it should be broken down with pickle juice).
   d. box for the labels and a box for the lids.
   e. a box with a sponge (like the type you would use to wet a stamp).
   f. 3 × trays (one large one).

Props
1 Please note, we will require a lighter wooden bucket than the one we have in rehearsals.
2 Please note, we require 6 x crates.

Wardrobe
1 Please note, a loop is required on Bryman's [factory owner] coat or trousers to hold a conductor's baton.

Once the rehearsals have started, weekly **production meetings** or progress meetings, are usually called and chaired by the stage manager and provide an opportunity for feedback about any aspect of the production. The acting company is normally not required to attend these meetings. The purpose of the meeting is to check that all work is progressing at a steady pace, that deadlines are met and budgets are met. The meetings should be recorded and the minutes circulated. **Production schedules** vary considerably and the order of events is determined by what is possible both logistically and financially, given the requirements of the set, venue, and scenographic team. Here is the fit-up schedule for *You're Thinking About Doughnuts*:

Saturday 25 May

10.30 p.m.	Strike previous show and LX rig Doughnuts [this work continues through the night]
08.00 a.m.	Building Close

Sunday 26 May

2.00 p.m.	Rig flys
6.00 p.m.	Building Close

Monday 27 May

9.00 a.m.	Stage crew and Construction fit-up for Doughnuts
1.00 p.m.	Lunch
2.00 p.m.	Continue
6.00 p.m.	Dinner
7.00 p.m.	Continue
11.00 p.m.	Set to be complete, paint call
6.00 a.m.	Building Close

Tuesday 28 May

9.00 a.m.	Dead all bars
11.00 a.m.	LX to focus
1.00 p.m.	Lunch/sound session
2.00 p.m.	LX to continue
5.30 p.m.	LX to finish focus/set for lighting session
6.30 p.m.	Lighting session
10.45 p.m.	Lighting to be complete
11.00 p.m.	All calls end

Wednesday 29 May

10.00 a.m.	Half-hour call for technical rehearsal
10.35 a.m.	Technical session 1
1.15 p.m.	Technical session 1 to finish
1.30 p.m.	Lunch
2.30 p.m.	Technical session 2
6.15 p.m.	Technical session 2 to finish
6.30 p.m.	Dinner
7.30 p.m.	Technical session 3
10.15 p.m.	Technical session 3 to finish
10.30 p.m.	All calls end

Thursday 30 May

9.30 a.m.	Half-hour call for technical rehearsal
10.05 a.m.	Technical session 4
1.15 p.m.	Technical rehearsal to be complete

1.30 p.m.	Lunch
2.30 p.m.	Technical notes on stage
5.30 p.m.	Set for dress rehearsal
6.00 p.m.	Dinner
7.00 p.m.	Continue setting for dress rehearsal
7.25 p.m.	Half-hour call for dress rehearsal
8.00 p.m.	Dress rehearsal
10.30 p.m.	All calls end

Friday 31 May

9.00 a.m.	Technical notes on stage
12.00 noon	Set for dress rehearsal
12.30 p.m.	Lunch
1.30 p.m.	Half-hour call
2.05 p.m.	Dress rehearsal
4.40 p.m.	Company break set for preview
5.00 p.m	Dinner
6.25 p.m.	Half-hour call
7.00 p.m.	Preview
10.15 p.m.	All calls end

Saturday 1 June

9.00 a.m.	Technical notes on stage
12.00 noon	Lunch
1.00 p.m.	Set for performance
1.25 p.m.	Half-hour call
2.00 p.m.	Performance
4.40 p.m.	Company break set for first night
5.00 p.m.	Dinner
6.00 p.m.	Set for first night
6.25 p.m.	Half-hour call
7.00 p.m.	First night

You will notice in the schedule that time is allowed for food breaks and preparation. The calls are dependent on overtime payments; however, many theatres do not call staff who have not had an eleven-hour break from the end of a previous call.

As the schedule illustrates, during the fit-up all the physical aspects of set, lighting and sound are brought together. Organisation and clever use of the time available is essential as some staff overlap in their duties and skill areas. Every theatre building or public performance space should have a code of practice which is accessible to all those who use the building and its facilities. All European theatres adhere to specific codes of practice which have been drawn up to protect theatre workers from long hours, poor working conditions and ultimately dangerous practice (see p. 1).

The **technical rehearsal** is the full run of the play, when all the technical elements are added and cues are positioned in the prompt copy. It is overseen by the stage manager, who, in liaison with the director, starts and stops scenes as appropriate and checks that all departments understand the DSM's instructions. Though a rehearsal of technical problems and operations, it must be played by the actors at performance pitch and tempo to enable the designers and director to time cues and movements to match the action. As soon as there is a need to stop the run of a section or scene, the stage manager will call the actors to halt the performance. Then re-cueing or any other problems can be solved or discussed. Then the stage manager will give the company a cue from where to restart the action. These rehearsals are often long and tiring and require patience and an understanding of what the management is trying to achieve. This is the time when actors need to check difficult exits, costume changes and any practical props. Cutting **cue-to-cue** allows the stage manager to 'fast forward' the text where no technical action needs to be rehearsed. This short-cutting has to be agreed by the director and designers and can speed up the rehearsal.

The **dress rehearsal** is run as if it were a performance. The stage management schedule for a 7.30 p.m. performance is as follows: the stage manager and technical team will set up and do checks for the performance at 5.55 p.m., an hour before the half-hour call. As each performer arrives he or she must sign in on a list posted at the stage door by the stage manager. At the half-hour call, which is 6.55 p.m., the stage manager checks that all the company has arrived, and then liaises with the front-of-house manager and the technicians and operators that all is in order for opening the house to the public. Before requesting the pre-set lighting state, which is the first lighting state the audience will see when they enter the auditorium, the stage manager asks for complete blackout in the theatre. This is to check that the only lights on are emergency lighting and

Health & Safety

Some good practice guidelines are listed below. **High risk** activities involve the use of machine tools and other equipment capable of inflicting serious injury; work with electrical equipment at dangerous voltages; working with heavy loads or weights, for example flying, securing large pieces of scenery, etc.; working on ladders or overhead catwalks at heights in excess of two metres. You should take great care when undertaking any of these tasks and wear hard hats when people are working overhead. Use harnesses and other safety equipment for working at heights. If you have not been trained to use specific pieces of equipment, wait for supervision or instruction.

Medium risk activities involve working with hand tools, including saws and chisels, making props, where varnish, glazes and spray paints might be in use and the use of resins and fast setting adhesives. For these activities you should wear masks, goggles and protective clothing such as gloves and overalls.

Even **low risk** activity, where no obvious hazard is involved, should be undertaken with care. This kind of work might involve the use of computer terminals, recording and playback of video and audio equipment, use of editing suites, etc. You should not undertake any of these activities if you have been drinking or using other substances for recreational use. You can be disciplined and ultimately removed from your job if you are using equipment for which you are not capable or have not been trained.

exit boxes. It allows the stage manager to check any working lights, such as those on props tables, making sure they are not throwing light onto the stage. Only after this has been completed should the pre-set and house lights go up. After this, no working lights should be switched on until the end of the performance when the audience has left the auditorium. The DSM makes a half-hour call, either by public address system or by going to each dressing room. They must also make sure the technicians are aware of all the calls. After the half-hour has been made no personnel are allowed in the front-of-house areas. The calls given by the DSM are as follows:

Ladies and gentlemen of the Doughnuts company, this is your half-hour call. Thirty minutes please, thank you. (6.55 p.m.)

Ladies and gentlemen of the Doughnuts company, this is your quarter-hour call. Fifteen minutes please, thank you. (7.10 p.m.)

Ladies and gentlemen of the Doughnuts company, this is your five-minute call. Five minutes please, thank you. (7.20 p.m.)

Ladies and gentlemen of the Doughnuts company, this is your beginners call for Act 1. Beginners please, thank you. (7.25 p.m.)

On the call for beginners, the company and all the technicians and operators go to their positions for the beginning of the show. When stage management is sure that everyone is in position, the DSM puts everyone on **standby**. The standby is the warning given just before a cue and is usually prefixed by the department name. They then wait to receive **front-of-house clearance** – the confirmation that all members of the audience are in and seated. The DSM can then start the show with the first cue, which may be lighting; for example, to take house lights out or perhaps a **cue light** to an actor to go on stage. A red cue light is used for standby, green for go. This is particularly useful when non-verbal cueing is required for actors, or for operators who need to be clear of headphones and leads, like sound operators and flys.

In addition to the backstage calls, the DSM is required to give **front-of-house calls** at five minutes, three minutes, two minutes and one minute before the performance begins, and which take the form: 'Ladies and gentlemen, welcome to Nottingham Playhouse, tonight's performance of *You're Thinking About Doughnuts* will begin in five minutes, five minutes please, thank you.' The DSM may also give an announcement to say when the house is initially open and people are able to take their seats.

After each performance the DSM completes a **show report**, which details what went wrong in performance with respect to actors, operators and technicians. The report also usually documents the kind of reception the performance received from the audience, as the example below illustrates.

SHOW REPORT

Distribution List: Director, Artistic Director, Production Manager, Props, Stage Management, Technical Manager, Publicity, Chief Electrician, Prompt Copy, Administration.

Production: *You're Thinking About Doughnuts*, no. 12

DSM: Deborah Constable; audience no. 602

	[curtain] UP	[curtain] DOWN	TIME
Act 1	10.02	11.02	60 minutes
Interval	11.02	11.21	19 minutes
Act 2	11.21	12.09	48 minutes

Total playing time: 1 hour 48 minutes
Total running time: 2 hours 07 minutes

SM: Jo Rawlinson, Stuart Lambert, Michael Dennis,
LX operator: Adam Rudd
Sound operator: Richard Mason
Stage technician: Michael Bannister
Flys: Richard Statham
Dressers: Clare Pegg, Jess Williams

REMARKS:
1 LX Q [cue] 27 late, DSM error
2 Mr Joy was very early jumping into Mr Lemkin in the Stonemen scene.
3 The children [in the audience] said 'Hi' when Elvis said ' Hiya fellas'.
4 The LX box was very cold this morning.
5 All the children screamed at Skelly [the skeleton] grabbing Frank's neck.
6 The Fly – the line for the proboscis got caught on the hairs. Mr Lemkin released it.
7 Some girls shouted 'Go girl!' during Marilyn's song.

Very responsive audience.
Good show, 1 call taken.

Although stage management deals extensively with the management of the stage, hopefully you can see by the examples given that organisation is very much a part of the creative process. What you desire artistically can only be unlocked by organisation which empowers your ideas and other people's. The cueing of a show and the operation of cues are integral to the dynamic of any performance, and high production values which are achieved every night are part of the stage manager's role in the creation of the performance.

MARK-OUT EXERCISE

Make sure you show where the front of the stage starts and where the extreme seats of the auditorium are. Look at the ground plan in fig. 9.2 and try to put down the design as a mark-out on the floor of your rehearsal space. You will need a scale ruler with the correct scale to read the plan accurately. Measure the lines on the plan and mark out the rehearsal space using PVC tape. Use different colours to indicate different scenic features. There are two effective ways of doing this:

1 Find the centre of the space you are working in. Mark the centre with PVC tape. This is your centre line. There should be a corresponding centre line on your plan. If not, find the centre on the plan and mark that in also. Your plan and space should correspond to these lines. Now measure out from the centre line up or down the centre line to either your furniture or the walls of your set to find where the lines should be on the floor. Mark the spots with some chalk and then join up your marks with the coloured PVC tape. This is the easiest method if you are on your own.

2 If you are working with a number of people, you can have one person reading off the measurements from the plan using the scale ruler and two people using two measuring tapes. Hammer a nail into the floor at the front of the playing area (also known as the setting line). This is usually just upstage of the house curtain and parallel to the front of the stage. It is the line from which the positions for scenery are measured. One nail should be at the extreme edge of your playing area stage right, the other on extreme stage left. Hook the end of each tape over the respective nail. As you stand on the stage facing the audience your left is stage left (sl), and your right is stage right (sr). The place on the playing area nearest the audience is downstage (ds) and the place furthest away from the audience is upstage (us). Now measure from the points of your playing area on the plan and read off your measurement to the first piece of set or furniture. Then read off this measurement on the tape measure. By using both measurements from sr and sl the two readings should give you the exact spot for the first edge or corner of your set. The tapes therefore cross at the correct reading of each. Mark the floor at the axis of the tapes, that is, where the two tapes across, with chalk or tape and then join up with tape as in example 1).

Remember – us, ds, sl, and sr are the ways in which theatre workers communicate direction to one another. These are important codes, as they will avoid any confusion about the direction of people, objects or lights. They are determined by you imagining that you are on the stage facing the audience.

CHAPTER 10

Multimedia Technology

Throughout this book I have tried to stress the importance of plot and aesthetic content over indiscriminate use of technology. In his *New Media in Late 20th-Century Art*, Michael Rush provides a useful insight: 'As in any technology-driven medium, the most dynamic work occurs when the technology catches up with the visions of the artists, or, conversely artists catch up with the technology' (1999: 192). In this chapter I wish to look at the impact of multimedia art on theatre.

In the theatre created by Robert Lepage and his company Ex Machina and the performance work of Laurie Anderson there are numerous opportunities for the collaboration between technicians, actors and musicians. In fact, this form of theatre relies on that interaction. However, in every case the success of the work is based on the relevance of the effect to the common aim – which is communicating with the audience. For example, in her adaptation of *Moby Dick*, Laurie Anderson's use of video screens and computer images is part of the artwork of the stage, allowing a dynamic set of images to be presented in a novel way. The aesthetic worked because it offered a coherent design choice which was augmented throughout the performance and was used as a subtle tool of communication. In this multimedia production, Anderson integrated the computer images with original pieces of music, composed for electric violin and other electronic instruments, choreographed sequences, and song.

This kind of work was, in fact, in operation for most of the twentieth century, and was very much led by the available technology. However, then as now, these technologies are only as inventive as the theatre practitioners who use them.

In recent years the use of television screens in live performance as another stimulus for the audience has produced mixed responses. I believe, however, that when such a device succeeds in communicating the artist's message, its use is vindicated.

Projection

As discussed in Chapter 6, there are a number of means of projection and mediums onto

---

Robert Lepage (1957–)

French-Canadian director working in large multimedia formats. His company Ex Machina specialise in media-based theatre works; for example, *Polygraph* (1990), *Needles and Opium* (1992), *Elsinore* (1995), and *The Seven Streams of the River Ota* (1996).

Laurie Anderson (1947–)

A musician and artist who creates multidisciplinary art. Examples of her performance work are *Automotive Duets on Ice* (1972); *Talk Normal* tour (1987–8); *Empty Places* (1989) première, Spoleto Festival (Charlestone, SC); *Empty Places* tour (1990), *Halcyon Days* (1992); *An Evening With Laurie Anderson* (1994); *The Nerve Bible* (1995); *Dal Vivio* (1998) and *Moby Dick* (2000).

Projection

Experimentation with lights and mirrors to produce projected images has taken place since 1646, when Athanasius Kircher (1601–80) published his research in Rome in 1646. Kircher's system relied on the reflection from a mirror, with sunlight or candlelight used as the source, focused with a bi-convex lens. The Phantasmagoria introduced in 1802 by Paul de Philipsthal were exhibited at the Lyceum Theatre in London. The event showed phantoms and apparitions of the dead. These images were back projected and so the result was all the more effective, as the mechanisms for projection were hidden from audience view. In 1838 British chemist John Henry Pepper (1821–1900), director of the Royal Polytechnic Institution in London, demonstrated the ability of light to be reflected several times. The experiment used a person standing in the orchestra pit illuminated by a lantern. The reflection was picked up in a piece of glass and then was angled onto a pane of glass, which was suspended on stage. This effect has since become known as Pepper's Ghost, even though the idea was originally Henry Dirk's, who sold the patent to Pepper.

which an image can be projected. The surface can be a solid structure, a cloth, or indeed the performers themselves. Screens can be set at any angle depending on the overall desired effect and use of the performance space. It is worth bearing in mind from the outset that few theatres will have projection equipment to suit all production requirements and there is a need, if you are touring, to supply all aspects of the projection equipment. The design and making of projection images should not be started until a clear understanding of the stage design has been agreed upon. In mediums such as slide and film it becomes very expensive to make mistakes which are due to lack of planning. This planning needs to include the actual position of the projector – whether it is hung or placed on another structure – and whether you are projecting from behind the projection surface or in front of it. Projectors are often heavy pieces of equipment and require appropriate rigging.

The choice of back projection or front projection will have different impacts on your stage space. The former will allow the projections to be placed upstage (and therefore the beams will not cross the performers' path) and avoids shadows being cast on the images. However, the stage space for performance will be diminished in order to provide the projector with enough distance to achieve a good-sized image. Usually the image size should be similar to the aperture of viewing for the audience. For instance, if the proscenium opening is 10 metres then you are likely to want to fill this space and mask with borders to the edges. If front projection is used, then the movement of scenery and people in front of the screen must be taken into account, because this movement will disrupt the projected image. In some cases, of course, this disruption may be a desired effect.

There is a limit to the size of image that is possible from a given distance from projector to screen. If you can not create the size of image you want from one projector, you may need to consider splitting the image into a series of images and projecting them with a number of projectors which then need to be lined up to make the full image. The basic principle of projecting remains the same, regardless of the projection medium being used (slide, video, computer image, and so on). A calculation for image size follows:

- **Focal length** (distance from centre of beam to point of image location) = F
- **Slide size** (width of slide) = O
- **Distance from screen** (distance from projector to screen location) = D
- **Picture size** (size of projected image) = B

$$F = \frac{O \times D}{B + O}$$

$$F = \frac{35 \text{ mm} \times 4000 \text{ mm}}{7000 \text{ mm} + 35 \text{ mm}}$$

then, F = 19.9
therefore, a lens size of 20 mm.

The choice of projector will be based on the number of slides you need to show. A carousel projector can hold up to eighty slides, whereas a Pani Projector BP4 can take only fifteen. Another consideration is the amount of light emitted by each machine; the carousel, for example, will produce a weaker light output.

Video and film projection allows movement on screen to be juxtaposed with live performance. **Laterna Magika** is just one method by which this effect has been achieved. Devised by Alfred Radok (1914–1976) and Josef Svoboda (1920–) in the late 1950s, this method consists of the integration of live performance with film projections of the performers. Svoboda's work is based on a metaphoric, rather than a realistic, approach to design. He recognised that set and lights form an organic, dynamic component of production. Although the use of the technique has degenerated into tourist entertainment in the Czech Republic, where it began, it was once used to great artistic effect in productions at the National Theatre in Prague. Contemporary British companies have also used these ideas to great effect. One notable comic use of film projection and live performance was Lip Service's 1994 production, *B-Road Movie* where two women performers portrayed Laurel and Hardy live on stage, while a film of Laurel and Hardy played behind them. The two performers were then seen to be dancing with Laurel and Hardy and reacting to the dialogue in the film.

The formats for film are 16 mm, 35 mm and 70 mm. The format will define the dimensions of the projector; the wider the film, the more light will pass through it. The most common format to use in conjunction with live performance is 16 mm, simply because it is easier to use and does not require extra features like ventilation and three-phase electricity

Pani Projector BP4

Ludwig Pani, synonymous with scenic projection, set up his company in 1930. This projector is the company's main product and uses a 4 kW lamp. The projector was first used in 1973 at the Bayreuth Festival, the annual music festival which performs Wagner's music-dramas at the Festival Theatre, built in 1876 for the first complete performance of the *Ring Cycle*.

supplies for the projector. If you are back projecting film, you will need to use a mirror to reverse bounce the projection, as film cannot be reversed in the same way that slides can.

The use of video projection can be effective, using either a small projector or a large Barco Projector. Video can also be projected using single television monitors or banks of monitors which form a video wall. Computer originated projection can be achieved via a data projector, either of the small lecture kind or the Barco Projector, most of which have a computer input. This means that designs for images can be drawn on computer programmes and then operated from the computer to appear on screen. The interface of live performance with the digital images will also be mostly dependent on the appropriateness of the form to the content. Computer software packages, offering a range of drawing facilities and image layers, can be projected quite easily. However, they must still be checked against the overall scenic arrangement and should not be considered a useful aesthetic in their own right. There is nothing impressive about computer projection, or any other form of multimedia imaging, unless it is delivering a creative response in harmony with the message of the scenographic team.

Reclaiming spectacle in the twenty-first century

The efficacy of spectacle in theatre is based on its ability to manipulate our emotional response to theatrical events. The impact of spectacle and the spectacular cannot be understood without first trying to define what it is we mean by the word 'spectacle'. A dictionary definition gives: 'strange and interesting, an impressive, grand or dramatic show, designed to impress; magnificent and important'. The word 'grand' suggests 'large', and 'dramatic' suggests a sense of the striking or effective, that which has some kind of emotional impact or is performed in a flamboyant way.

The power of the spectacular on the spectator is an individualistic moment, even though the audience often gives a unified reaction. As Susan Bennett explains in *Theatre Audiences: A Theory of Production and Reception*: 'While audience homogeneity would seem to be most likely, it is worth remembering the vulnerability of that unified response. That audiences generally concur as to what is a good play and what is bad merely evidences aesthetic codes as culturally determined' (1994: 165). The spectacular effect, whether it is delivered at a certain moment or throughout a complete performance, is designed specifically to provoke the desired response. Theatre practitioners work as actors do, knowing how to manipulate their audiences, and like some actors, some makers of theatre are more subtle than others at concealing the mechanisms for evoking certain responses. In other words, the techniques of production, like techniques of acting, can be crude cliché or an art form. The former has frequently been associated with popular productions with an eye to commercial success, and as such has received adverse critical attention. It is true that during the last two decades of the twentieth century, lighting and stagecraft was used, as Bennett says, 'to heighten the theatrical experience for the audience' (1994: 119). In 1995 set designer Bob Crowley recalled some problems brought about by this sudden explosion of stagecraft:

In the 80s, designers had the responsibility for turning rather dodgy musicals into pieces of theatre. These musicals weren't inherently theatrical and they depended for their lifeblood on the designer, because nothing else was happening. What's happened since has probably been a bit of a backlash ... I was worried that all we'd done in the 80s was to replace one boring set of clichés with another set.

(RNT, 1993: 19–20)

Theatre that is flamboyantly manipulative has been judged as a lesser art form, not because less craft is involved in creating these works, but because the production does not disguise the means of manipulation. However, it would be unfair and unwise to view all spectacle as purely gratuitous. Crowley's comment points up the need to determine the nature of the theatrical event, and technology's relationship to that event. Whether or not an audience responds to an event will be determined by the choice of techniques the theatre-makers elect to follow. Without doubt, manipulation is part of their skill. However, when the technology inherent in this process is revealed rather than integrated into the event, the result is not only a badly designed effect within the context of the overall production but a removal of the possibility of the audience experiencing its full potential. In other words, the efficacy of the technology to produce an emotional response in an audience is evident only if the technology combines with other features of the production to create a cohesive signal to that audience.

At the start of the twenty-first century, both in the world of theatre and in the world of academia, attitudes towards technical theatre have changed considerably. No longer is technology considered a radical force and one to be feared. A clearer analysis of the use of technology as both exciting and pragmatic has calmed an earlier knee-jerk reaction which claimed that the use of technology stymied new writing and was the downfall of 'good' theatre. It is now widely acknowledged that it is the mass production of theatre, and not technology *per se*, that will lead to stagnation; and that without technology there can be no future experimentation in the theatre.

Technical theatre is significant and powerful in the hands of those creative practitioners who embrace it. Ultimately, the poetic of scenography cannot be extricated from the total theatre event, once the audience has viewed that event, but like poetry, the resonant images continue to reverberate, long after the poem has been read.

CHAPTER 11

Exercises

You should now be able to embark on a number of exciting projects. The short exercises in the specialist chapters have hopefully enabled you to understand some detailed aspects of technical theatre. The multiple choice questions below are to test your general technical knowledge, and you can apply your practical skills to completing the Flat Project on p. 136.

Multiple Choice Questions

(Answers on p. 137)

1 A gobo is
   a) method of hanging a lantern
   b) a metal shape that can be put in a lantern and projected
   c) a type of lantern

2 A gobo fits in
   a) a fresnel
   b) a profile
   c) a flood

3 dB stands for
   a) do brighter
   b) decibel
   c) Dombey Boom

4 A dresser is
   a) a member of staff who helps with quick changes
   b) a piece of furniture used in quick changes
   c) a type of hanger used for quick changes

5 UK mains electrical wiring is coded
   a) purple, orange, red/earth, neutral, live
   b) red, brown, yellow/live, neutral, earth
   c) brown, blue, yellow/green/live, neutral, earth

6 Current is measured in
   a) cms
   b) amps
   c) volts

7   The plugging order from a microphone to the reproduced sound would be
   a) mic desk amp speaker
   b) desk mic amp speaker
   c) amp mic desk speaker

8   SM means
   a) stage manager
   b) scenic maker
   c) scenic manager

9   A DSM is responsible for
   a) rehearsal prompt copy and cueing the show in the theatre
   b) collecting props and making props
   c) props budget and cue sheets

10   If you are standing on stage facing the audience, where is stage right?
   a) on your left
   b) on your right
   c) auditorium right

11   Upstage is
   a) nearest the audience
   b) furthest away from the audience
   c) stage left

12   To breakdown a costume means to
   a) shout at the actor who is wearing it
   b) to tear it into pieces
   c) make it look old and dirty

13   Sheets of plywood can be ordered in
   a) 8 feet × 2 feet
   b) 8 feet × 4 feet
   c) 4 feet × 6 feet

14   A rail is
   a) the vertical support of a flat
   b) the diagonal support of a flat
   c) the horizontal support of a flat

15   A flat can be held up by
   a) belt and braces
   b) a brace and weight
   c) a mace and weight

16   A cleat is
  a) the means of supporting a flat using rope
  b) the means of supporting a flat using a wooden peg
  c) the means of supporting a flat using a brick

17   A counterweight is
  a) a weight to stop a counter falling over
  b) part of a stage counter
  c) part of a flying system

18   The best glue for fabric is
  a) Size
  b) Araldite
  c) Copydex

19   The person responsible for the public in the theatre building is the
  a) FOH manager
  b) SM
  c) Artistic Director

20   The minimum gap between set and audience is
  a) 1.10 m
  b) 110 m
  c) 11.0 m

21   The 5 minute call to technical staff and actors for a show starting at 7.30pm would be
  a) 7.25
  b) 7.15
  c) 7.20

22   P – V x I means
  a) people = volume x interest
  b) power = volts x induction
  c) power = volts x amps

23   Muslin is
  a) a type of scenic cloth
  b) a cloth used as FOH tabs
  c) a religion

24   You would write information about lighting, sound and cueing in
  a) a prompt book
  b) a note book
  c) a rehearsal diary

25 What is size?
a) a form of glue
b) a measurement
c) a cloth

26 Masking is used to
a) hide your face
b) hide the wings from the audience
c) tape down the floor

27 A mark-out is
a) the price of props
b) a tape plan on the rehearsal floor of the outline of the set
c) a tape plan on the rehearsal floor of the theatre

28 What is a general cover?
a) a cloth to cover the stage
b) a patchy area of light
c) a complete wash of light to cover an area of the stage

29 What would be the correct fuse rating for a 1 kW lantern?
a) 10 amps
b) 5 amps
c) 15 amps

30 Flying irons are
a) boots to be worn on the fly floor
b) a method of flying scenery
c) a piece of ironmongery used for flying people

31 Who gives front-of-house clearance?
a) the ushers
b) stage manager
c) the FOH manager

32 Scenery is made non-flammable by applying
a) water
b) Flamebar
c) Flammable

33 A costume plot is
a) a plan of the costumes needed for the play
b) a description of quick changes
c) a design of a costume

34 Hose are
a) women's tights
b) men's tights
c) girl's tights

35 A swatch is
a) a small sample of fabric used for costume designs
b) a sample of fabric attached to costumes
c) a miniature of the whole costume

36 A mixer is
a) a desk for distributing sound
b) an amplifier
c) a type of plug

37 The duties of a wardrobe supervisor are
a) making and cutting of designed costumes
b) keeping the wardrobe tidy
c) supervising the washing of costumes

38 You would clean velvet by using
a) masking tape
b) a dry cleaning company
c) prewashing it in a washing machine

39 Goggles and gloves must be worn when
a) using electrical saws
b) when using all tools
c) when using hand saws

40 Hemp is
a) a cigarette
b) a type of prop
c) a rope

41 Computer lighting boards can
a) remember cues and play them back
b) design lighting plans
c) communicate with the DSM

42 Outriggers must always be used on a tallescope
a) to maintain balance and stability on uneven floors
b) to maintain lanterns on bars
c) to maintain access to difficult positions on stage

43 An omni-directional microphone picks up sound
    a) from two directions
    b) from a localised source
    c) from all directions

The Flat Project

The flat project will draw on all you have learned so far in terms of construction. It sets a task which allows you to do some research, design and development. In each of the technical arts sections there is information which will help you complete the exercise. You should apply all that you have learned about approaches to technical theatre to create a place to play, in which you can get-in, fit-up and perform, using a soundtrack and lighting cues. Don't forget to invite an audience so that you can get feedback on the environment you have created and the story you have told. Choose one of the two options to design, build and perform. You may choose your recording medium and the number of sources to be used to produce your designed soundscape. You may, for instance, complete one recording which plays throughout or produce effects of particular sounds which you operate within a time sequence determined by light changes and what you expect your audience to perceive from the performance. In either case you will operate and therefore perform using the soundtrack(s) and lighting cues you have created.

The Brief

Either

Research and design a flat, room, or space where:
The period is the 1930s and we are in a hot room, in a southern Mediterranean country. The space is light and airy, and very warm.

Or

Research and design a flat, room, or space where:
The space contains a chair, a form of flooring, a vase and a strange *oject d'art*. The environment is bohemian. The period is 1920.

Workshop and Construction
Make an 8 feet × 4 feet flat. Make a working drawing and design your space to contain it. How will it stand up? What does this scenic structure indicate to your audience?

Lighting and Sound
Try to give a sense of the passage of time. We need to feel the atmosphere of the room, what sounds are there, other than those made by people? Are there any noises outside the room? What lighting comes into the room and is there any artificial light? What time of

day is it? In order to complete this part of the project, you will have to learn how to plot on the lighting board and fit-up and run your sound effects.

Design
Research the period and write the narrative of what your audience will experience. Choose your materials carefully: the audience should have a sense of the owner of the room.

Stage Management
Gather the props you will need for dressing, practicals, etc. You will need to refer to your research to make sure that what you are presenting to your audience reflects the correct period.

Plans and Working Drawings
The flat will need working drawings. How will you make the joints? What kind of materials are you using? Is it a door flat, a window flat, a solid flat or some other kind of flat that you have designed? You will also need working drawings for any objects which you want to make for the room.

A major part of this exercise is time management, so you need to set yourself a performance date and other interim deadlines. Order your materials and start creating!

Answers to Multiple Choice Questions on pp. 131–6.

1b	2b	3b
4a	5c	6b
7a	8a	9a
10b	11b	12c
13b	14c	15b
16a	17c	18c
19a	20a	21c
22c	23a	24a
25a	26b	27b
28c	29b	30b
31c	32b	33a
34b	35a	36a
37a	38b	39a
40c	41a	42a
43c		

Bibliography and further reading

Chapter 1

Edstrom, P. (1990) *Why Not Theaters Made for People?* Varmdo, Sweden: Arena Theatre Institute Foundation. A clear mapping of the influence of Vedic thought on theatre building and the need to link the dimensions of a space to the nature of performance.

Gurr, A. and Orrell, J. (1989) *Rebuilding Shakespeare's Globe.* London: Weidenfeld and Nicolson. A comprehensive guide to the building of the Globe and the dramaturgy that developed.

Ham, R. (ed.) (1972) *Theatre Planning.* London: Architectural Press. A guide to the physical building of a theatre. Example plans of different styles and types of theatre performance space.

Lewis, J. (1990) *Art, Culture and Enterprise: The Politics of Art and Cultural Industries.* London: Routledge. A clear outline of the inter-relatedness of art, culture and financial constraints and the politics of art.

Mackintosh, I. (1992) *Architecture, Actor, and Audience.* London: Routledge. A theatre history of playhouses in Britain.

McLuhan, M. (2001) *The Medium is the Massage: An Inventory of Effects.* New York: Gingko Press. A theory of the impact of popular culture and the media on information.

Nagler, A.N. (1952) *A Source Book in Theatrical History.* New York: Dover Publications.

O'Doherty, B. (1999) *Inside the White Cube: The Ideology of the Gallery Space.* Santa Monica: University of California Press. A theory of the art gallery and the differing ways in which this can be used.

Pick, J. (1986) *Managing the Arts? The British Experience.* London: Rhinegold. Outlines arts administration practice in Britain, the way in which British theatre has been funded and the impact on the products which are created.

Rowell, G. and Jackson, A. (1984) *The Repertory Movement. A History of Regional Theatre in Britain.* Cambridge: Cambridge University Press. Outlines the rise of repertory theatres and the types of work that were developed in the regions of Britain.

Rowland, I. and Noble Howe, T. (eds.) (2001) *Vitruvius: Ten Books on Architecture.* London: Lockwood & Co. The ten books of Vitruvius translated from the Latin by Joseph Gwilt, to which is prefixed an inquiry into the principles of beauty in Grecian architecture by George, Earl of Aberdeen. This book sets out the main ideas that form the basis for theatre buildings and ideas of space and staging.

Serlio, S. (1996). *Sebastiano Serlio on Architecture.* New Haven: Yale University Press. This outlines the work of both Serlio and Vitruvius.

Sinclair, A. (1995) *Arts and Cultures: The History of the 50 years of the Arts Council of Great Britain*. London: Sinclair-Stevenson. A good overview of the Arts Council.

Strong, J. (1990) *Arts Council Guide to Building for the Arts*. London: Arts Council of Great Britain (ACGB). A guide to planning in the early 1990s.

Styan, J.L. (1996). *The English Stage: A History of Drama and Performance*. Cambridge: Cambridge University Press. A good text for undergraduates of theatre history.

Vasari, G. (1999) *Vasari on Theatre*. Carbondale, IL.: Southern Illinois University Press. A useful book showing the way in which art and theatre have been related. Vasari documents the period and contemporary Italian theories of art.

Walther White, E. (1975) *The Arts Council of Great Britain 1905–1985*. London: Davis-Poynter. This is an account based on personal experience by a former Assistant Secretary to CEMA and the Arts Council 1942–1971.

Witts, R. (1998) *Artist Unknown: The Alternative History of the Arts Council*. London: Little Brown. This history takes into account developments in artistic practice.

Chapter 2

Algarotti, F. (1767) *An Essay on the Opera*. London: L. Davis & C. Reymer. A treatise on ideas in opera production in the 18th century and how these might be improved.

Chapter 3

Arnott, B. (1975) *Towards A New Theatre: Edward Gordon Craig and Hamlet*. Ottawa: National Gallery of Canada. A discussion of new ideas for theatre performance.

Bablet, D. (1981) *Edward Gordon Craig*. London: Heinemann. A very good biography of the stage designer Gordon Craig.

Barnard, M. (1996) *Fashion as Communication*. London: Routledge. A theory of fashion in contemporary dress.

Fuerst, W.R and Hume, S.J. (1928) *Twentieth-Century Stage Decoration*. London: A.A. Knopf. An outline of the developments in style and theory of scenic presentations on stage. The history and theory has a companion volume of photographs and illustrations from productions.

Hollander, A. (1994) *Sex and Suits*. New York: Kodansha America. A discussion of gender and fashion.

Leacroft, (1973) *The Development of the English Playhouse*. London: Methuen. A history of the development of the built playing spaces for theatre in England.

Martin, R. (1988) *Fashion and Surrealism*. London: Thames & Hudson. An account of the development of surrealism within fashion.

Proctor, R. and Lew, J. (1984) *Surface Design on Fabric*. Seattle: University of Washington Press. Interesting design ideas with fabric.

Rudnitsky, K. (1988) *Russian and Soviet Theatre: Tradition and the Avant Garde*. London: Thames & Hudson. A history of the development of artistic genres in the theatre. This is a very good record of Russian theatre with photographs.

Simonson, L. (1950) *The Art of Scenic Design: A Pictorial Analysis of Stage Setting and its Relation to Theatrical Production*. New York: Harrap. A guide to American set design

Simonson, L. (1963) *The Stage is Set.* New York: Theatre Art Books. A guide to American theatre with some very good photographs.

Stanislavksy, C. (1980) *My Life In Art.* Methuen: London. The autobiography of Constantin Sergeevich Stanislavsky.

Stanley, H. (1991) *Flat Pattern Cutting and Modelling for Fashion.* Cheltenham: Stanley Thornes. A guide to the practicalities of pattern making.

Wilson, E. (1996) *Adorned in Dreams: Fashion and Modernity.* London: Virago. A discussion of the theories of fashion and development of critical thinking.

RNT, 1993, Platform Papers 4 . Designers: Bob Crowley, Jocelyn Herbert, John Napier. Royal National Theatre, London. A transcript of interviews given at the Royal National Theatre with designers who had recently worked there.

Chapter 4

Payne, D.R. (1993) *Scenographic Imagination.* Carbondale: Southern Illinois University Press. A clear outline of the role of scenography and the work of the scenographer.

Payne, D.R. (1985) *Theory and Craft of the Scenographic Model.* Carbondale: Southern Illinois University Press. A clear guide to the process of model-making and the tools to create certain effects.

van Buitenen, J.A.B. (trans.) (1973) *The Mahabharuta.* Chicago & London: University of Chicago Press. The Indian epic tale which forms the basis for most Asian mythic stories.

Chapter 5

Aston, E. (1991) *Theatre As Sign System.* London: Routledge. An A-level reader on semiotics and performance.

Barthes, R. (1984) *Image Music Text.* London: Flamingo. A theory of image, music and text as it relates to the creation of these art works. Barthes outlines the importance of the raw nature of culture and the impact of the means of production on the product created.

Bentley, E. (1997) *The Theory of the Modern Stage: An Introduction to Modern Theatre and Drama.* New York & London: Applause. A good theoretical handbook for undergraduates.

Esslin, M. (1987) *The Field of Drama: How Signs of Drama Create Meaning on Stage and Screen.* London: Methuen. An introductory guide to the ideas of semiotics without too much jargon.

Jung, C. G. (1971) *Psychological Reflections: A New Anthology of his Writings: 1905–1961.* Selected and edited by Jolande Jacobi in collaboration with R.F.C. Hull. London: Routledge and Kegan Paul. An overview of Jung's writings.

Kershaw, B. (1992) *The Politics of Performance: Radical Theatre as Cultural Intervention.* London: Routledge.

Pavis, P. (1992) *Theatre at the Crossroads of Culture.* London: Routledge. A discussion of culture and inter-culturalism.

Rudlin, J. (1986) *Jacques Copeau.* Cambridge: Cambridge University Press. An account of Copeau's life and work as a director

Sandford, M. (1995) *Happenings and Other Acts.* London: Routledge. An account of street performance, installations and spontaneous performances in non-theatre environments.

Taplin, O. (1978) *Greek Theatre in Action.* London: Methuen. A clear guide to Greek tragedy with a strong emphasis on performance

Volbach, W.R. (1968) *Adolphe Appia: Prophet of the Modern Theatre*: A Profile. Wesleyan University Press, edited and translated by Richard Beacham. A biography of Appia.

Volbach, W.R. (1989) *Adolphe Appia, Essays, Scenarios, and Designs*, edited Richard C. Beacham. Ann Arbor: UMI Research Press. Appia's own works and ideas with a clear commentary from Richard Beacham.

Wallis, M. and Shepherd, S. (1998) *Studying Plays.* London: Arnold. An introduction to the methods and terminology used in the analysis of dramatic texts.

Wright, E. (1989) *Post-Modern Brecht: A Representation.* London: Routledge. A thorough discussion of Brecht and the impact of his theatre in the context of a postmodern aesthetic.

Chapter 6

Holt, M. (1988) *Scene Painting and Prop Making.* Oxford: Phaidon. A first guide to principles of both scene painting and prop making.

Chapter 7

Fraser, N. (1999) *Stage Lighting Design: A Practical Guide.* Marlborough: Crowood. A thorough guide to the practice of stage lighting design with exercises.

Reid, F. (1992) *The Stage Lighting Handbook.* London: A & C Black. A classic guide to the principles of stage lighting.

Chapter 8

Fraser, N. (1993) *Lighting and Sound.* London: Phaidon Press. A combination of basic principles for sound and light for the stage.

Millerson, G. (1995) *The Use of Microphones.* Focal Press. A clear guide to the way microphones work.

Walne, G. (1981) *Sound for theatres: A Basic Manual.* Eastbourne: John Offord. A clear outline of the problems and pitfalls in quite technical language.

Chapter 9

Menear, P. (1988) *Stage Management and Theatre Administration.* Oxford: Phaidon. A guide to the systems of stage management and administration.

Reid, F. (2001) *The Staging Handbook*, London: A.& C. Black. A guide to staging objects and techniques.

Chapter 10

Bennett, S. (1997) *Theatre Audiences.* London: Routledge.

Pilbrow, R. (1997) *Stage Lighting Design: The Art, the Craft, the Life.* London: Nick Hern Books. A guide to stage lighting with designers' comments. Although written from a stage lighting perspective, the principles of projection are also discussed.

Rush, M. (1999) *New Media in Late 20th Century Art.* London: Thames and Hudson.

Simpson, R.S. (1992) *Effective Audio Video: A User's Handbook.* Oxford: Focal Press. A guide to using slides and moving images.

Walne, G. (1995) *Projection for the performing arts.* Oxford: Focal Press. A history and theory of projection in all mediums.

Lighting and Sound International: the entertainment technology monthly. The Professional Lighting and Sound Association (PLASA), Eastbourne. An industry magazine which illustrates the latest equipment for sound and lighting in the entertainment industries.

Index